The KISS ME Curse
A Comedy in Two Acts

By
Vin Morreale, Jr.

Cover Design by
Stephen Koller - SJKoller.com

ISBN 978-0-9991473-5-1

academyartspress.com

All Rights Reserved.
Copyright © 2019 by Vin Morreale, Jr.

The KISS ME Curse
A Comedy in Two Acts

By
Vin Morreale, Jr.

CAST

Narrator/Mr. LaGrange	folksy manner, but poetic
Angie Buckner	slightly frazzled widow
Dale Watterson	mild-mannered dreamer
Snyder/Waiter #2	tough-talking bartender
Jared	dim-witted teen
Maggie/Sister Mary Margaret	Angie's former classmate
Waddy Peytona/Waiter #1	slick fertilizer salesman
Sligo Newcastle/Father Lawrence	mob boss/blind priest

The KISS ME Curse
A Comedy in Two Acts

By
Vin Morreale, Jr.

SETTING

ACT ONE

Scene 1: Flyaway Lounge
Scene 2: Angie's Apartment
Scene 3: Pewee Valley High
Scene 4-6: Angie's Apartment

ACT TWO

Scenes 1-3: Angie's Apartment
Scene 4: Father Lawrence Berg's office

> For royalty information and permission to use this play in a performance, please email vin@academyarts.com

THE KISS ME CURSE

ACT ONE
Scene 1

AT RISE: Lights come up on a dimly lit, simply dressed set with unadorned, neutral color walls. Three small circular tables are staggered at comfortable intervals, each with chairs, suggesting a café or lounge area. A small bar stands Stage Right. Most of the area is gently bathed in shadows, except a sharp-edged blue spotlight Downstage Center.

(Our NARRATOR steps from the shadows. He is a middle-aged man with pleasant smile and folksy nature. He scowls at the blue spotlight without stepping into it.)

NARRATOR. No. That won't do. Won't do at all.

(He steps into the spotlight and addresses the audience.)

NARRATOR. Blue is absolutely the wrong color. It suggests coldness and death. And though we will see more than our share of death tonight, this is a comedy. Comedies should be brighter and easier on the eyes, don't you think?

(The spotlight turns from blue to yellow-white.)

NARRATOR. Ah, much better. I feel more alive already. And since this is also a love story, perhaps a touch of crimson, like the soft warm blush of scarlet on a young lover's cheek…

(The spot warms with a splash of red added to the yellow-white.)

NARRATOR. That's it. Now we are in the mood for our little play. You should always be in the mood. *(Shields his eyes to peer into the audience.)* I can tell that gentleman in the center row is in the mood already. I suggest the lady beside him keep a close eye on his hands. Yes, you, sir. We prefer to keep our entertainment on stage.

NARRATOR. What was I saying before I was distracted by Mr. Frisky Hands there? Ah, yes. Being in the mood. And what mood, you might ask? Well, *delight*, since our goal is to make you laugh. *Romance and regret*, since we will see love won and lost. Then *delight* once more, as we will end on a happy note. This being a comedy after all.

Delight. Romance. Regret. And Delight again. All the components of a well-lived life, rich with experience, wouldn't you say? At least that's what I'd say, and since I am the Narrator standing on this stage, I suppose I'm in the perfect position to say it. But we have a story to tell, and it is time to get right to it.

Where to begin? As in life, we often fail to recognize those important, pivotal moments. So perhaps we should let our tale take off at the airport…

LOUDSPEAKER VOICE. Southwest Flight 42 Now Arriving at Gate 17.

NARRATOR. *(Chuckles.)* See what I did there? Take off at the airport… *(Calls offstage.)* Gentlemen, if you please…

> *(STAGE HANDS enter from various sides of the stage. They carry signs and props, as they dress the set to look like an airport lounge. A SIGN reading "GATES A 1-20" is placed on the STAGE LEFT wall. Another sign on a stand reads 'BAGGAGE CLAIM' with an arrow pointing off STAGE RIGHT. A few toy airplanes are placed on the tables. Finally, a sign reading "FLYAWAY LOUNGE" is positioned UPSTAGE CENTER.)*

LOUDSPEAKER VOICE. The yellow zone is for loading and unloading of passengers only…

NARRATOR. Are you getting the picture?

> *(DALE WATTERSON saunters on SR, rolling a piece of carry-on luggage.*
>
> *He looks around the empty lounge, nods at the Narrator, then takes a seat at the small table DL.)*

NARRATOR. Let me introduce Mr. Dale Watterson. Single. Thirty-two. He runs a small antique shop in Pewee Valley, Kentucky. Dale is an IU fan, which is why he is sitting alone here at the Louisville Airport. And since Indiana lost today, he isn't in the mood to talk sports, or talk to anyone for that matter. But that will soon change.

(DALE flags down one of the STAGE HANDS, who takes off his Pilot's uniform jacket, unfurls an apron, and transforms into WAITER #1.)

DALE. Makers Mark on the rocks.

WAITER #1. Right away, sir.

(Waiter #1 moves to the bar to pour the drink. Dale scribbles on his cocktail napkin.)

NARRATOR. Like most of us, Dale had big plans for his life. Travel the world. Cure cancer. Eradicate poverty. Write the Great American Novel. And like most of us, none of his dreams panned out. Yet he chooses to remain hopeful, because that is his nature.

(WAITER #1 crosses back to the table. Hands Dale his drink.)

WAITER #1. Makers Mark on the rocks. Will there be anything else, sir?

DALE. *(Showing him the cocktail napkin scribbles.)* Just your opinion. I'm working on this idea for generating cheap electric power using radio waves, Ramen noodles, and discarded tinsel from Christmas trees. I haven't cracked the energy output and flammability issues yet, but I think I'm...

WAITER #1. I'm sorry, sir. But I have to get back to my other customers.

(They both take a long look around the deserted lounge.)

WAITER #1. I hope you understand.

DALE. Of course. Sorry to bother you.

(Waiter #1 exits, UL. Dale sighs and returns to his drink.)

NARRATOR. That's Dale. Always the dreamer. As the best people tend to be. But I suggest you don't get too attached to him, because Dale Watterson doesn't have long to live. Although he doesn't know it yet.

(ANGIE rushes on from Stage Right. She is in her early thirties, and extremely attractive. She carries with her a harried, haunted look, as she scans the lounge. Then sits at the furthest possible table from Dale.)

NARRATOR. Meet Angela Buckner. Thirty-three. And the reason Dale doesn't have long to live. But I suppose it's best to let these two tell the story themselves.

(Narrator exits UR. Angie catches Dale looking at her and quickly repositions her chair so her back faces him. As she does this, her purse falls to the floor.)

DALE. Excuse me. Excuse me, Miss?

ANGIE. Don't even think it.

DALE. Huh?

ANGIE. I'm not available, okay?

DALE. Available for what?

ANGIE. Available for anything. Whatever you have in mind. So forget it. You don't want to fall in love with me. Trust me.

DALE. Fall in love with you?

ANGIE. Look. You're smitten. I know. It's my eyes. My hair. My smile. The graceful sweep of my neck. The soft, smooth elegance of my recently shaved legs. Best to get all that out of your head.

DALE. Your legs weren't in my head…

ANGIE. A butt man, huh? Well, mine's equally impressive, but since I'm sitting down, you'll have to take my word for it.

DALE. I only wanted to tell you…

ANGIE. Don't give up, do you? But believe me, it won't end well. Just move on. Get over me. Don't make this harder than it already is.

DALE. There's something wrong with you, isn't there?

ANGIE. Wrong with me? I'm not trying to pick up strange women in an airport lounge at midnight! What's the matter? The local meat market lose its appeal? Your subscription to Desperatesingles.com run out?

DALE. I'm not trying to pick you up. I just wanted to tell you that you dropped your purse.

ANGIE. Ha! That is the lamest pick-up line I've ever heard.

DALE. It's not a line. Your purse is on the floor.

(She notices the purse. Bends to pick it up.)

ANGIE. Oh, I'm sorry. I thought you were trying to….

DALE. I wasn't.

(She nods, turns her back to him again.)

DALE. But if I was….

ANGIE. *(Too quickly.)* I'm married.

DALE. Oh. I'm sorry.

ANGIE. My husband will be here any minute.

DALE. Terribly sorry.

ANGIE. Sorry that I'm married? Or sorry about how badly you just crashed and burned?

DALE. Honestly? Both.

ANGIE. Honesty and humility. That's refreshing.

DALE. I'll leave you alone then….

(He turns back to his drink. After a moment, she starts smacking her cheeks, moaning and wailing with obviously artificial sobs.)

DALE. Excuse me… Excuse me…

ANGIE. What now?! My purse is on my lap!

DALE. I just wanted to see if you are all right.

ANGIE. Of course, I'm all right. Don't I look all right?!

DALE. Honestly, no.

ANGIE. What is it with you and honesty, huh?

DALE. Sorry. I'll leave you alone.

ANGIE. You said that before. And we both know how that turned out!

DALE. Are you always this rude to people trying to be nice to you?

ANGIE. Honestly? No…

(Pause. Then she grabs her chair and drags it to his table. Sits.)

ANGIE. It's…it's my husband. I'm supposed to meet him in Baggage Hold.

DALE. I hope you don't mind me asking, but your husband… he's not beating you or anything, is he?

ANGIE. Anything but. He is hopelessly devoted to me.

DALE. Then…?

ANGIE. I'd rather not talk about it.

(She pulls her chair back to her own table. Dale returns to his drink. After a beat, she grabs her chair and again drags it to his table. Sits close beside him.)

ANGIE. It's just that he was always such a good man…

DALE. *Was* a good man.? And now he's…?

ANGIE. In Baggage Hold.

DALE. I see. *(Beat.)* Not really, but…

ANGIE. I don't know why I'm telling you this. I should know better.

DALE. It's okay. My friends tell me I'm a good listener. They prefer it to hearing me speak. My name is Dale, by the way. Dale Watterson.

ANGIE. Angie. Angie… *(Pauses. Thinks for a moment.)* Uh, Buckner.

DALE. You don't seem very sure.

ANGIE. My life is a mess. You wouldn't believe it.

DALE. Try me. Let's start over. You're married.

ANGIE. Chronically. And usually with bad results.

DALE. So he is not your first husband?

ANGIE. Not even close.

DALE. And he's down in Baggage Claim.

ANGIE. No, Baggage Hold.

DALE. You lost me.

ANGIE. No, I lost him. He's in a box. A coffin, actually. Down in Baggage Hold. We were on an extended honeymoon, when he…he…

DALE. On your honeymoon? That's awful! How did he die?

ANGIE. Smiling.

DALE. Poor thing. You must be devastated.

ANGIE. Not really. I'm used to it.

DALE. You are used to your husband dying?

ANGIE. Not this one, obviously. It was his first time, and…

(WAITER #2 enters, SL. Walks over to the table with a smirk.)

WAITER #2. May I get you a drink, madam?

ANGIE. No, thank you. I…

(Angie looks at the new Waiter's face and SCREAMS.)

ANGIE. AAAAAAHHHHH!!

DALE. Easy. It's only the waiter!

WAITER #2. That's right. I'm the waiter.

ANGIE. That's the problem!

DALE. The waiter is the problem?

ANGIE. Yes. I mean, no. *(Grasping for a reason.)* I…um have this condition.

DALE. What condition?

ANGIE. A dread fear of waiters. It's called…

WAITER #2. Can't wait to hear this.

ANGIE. Servingmanophobia.

DALE. Servingmanophobia?

ANGIE. It's a thing. At least, it's my thing. Now, please, go away. Get out of here!

WAITER #2. As you wish, Madam.

(Waiter #2 moves DR and begins to set the table.)

DALE. Uh, would you like to explain all that?

ANGIE. I'm sorry. I couldn't help it. It was his face.

DALE. That's a bit harsh. The guy is no Adonis, but I don't think he's that…

ANGIE. No. His face. I've seen him before.

DALE. Oh? You hang out in airport lounges waiting for your husband's body a lot?

ANGIE. More often than I'd like. Can I tell you something without you thinking I'm completely insane?

DALE. Might be a bit late for that. But give it a shot.

ANGIE. That waiter had my dead husband's face.

DALE. Oh, I can imagine how upsetting that would be! Seeing someone who looked like your late husband.

ANGIE. He didn't just look like my late husband. He had his face!

DALE. And we're back on the train to Crazy Town…

ANGIE. I knew you wouldn't understand.

DALE. I'm sorry. That was rude of me. What was your husband's name?

ANGIE. That one? Sammy, I think. No, Snyder. Yes, that was the name I was moaning when he…when he…

DALE. Smiled his last?

ANGIE. You can't imagine how long it took the embalmer to get that grin off his face. Not to mention his...

WAITER #2. *(Entering)* Check, sir?

ANGIE. AAAAAAHHHH!

WAITER #2. I realize our prices are high, but it is only one drink.

DALE. I'm sorry. She has recently experienced a personal tragedy. Her husband...

ANGIE. He knows all about it.

DALE. He does?

ANGIE. I'll be back in a moment.

(She grabs the Waiter's arm and marches him, DR.)

ANGIE. What are you doing here? You're only recently dead!

WAITER #2. Hey, nobody told me there was a time limit. One minute, I'm a newlywed looking for nookie with my new bride in Naples. Next thing I know, my body's in a box in Baggage Hold, and my spirit is serving drinks in the Flyaway Lounge!

ANGIE. I warned you this would happen.

WAITER #2. How was I supposed to believe you? Who could believe this?!

ANGIE. Marriages should be based on trust. That's the problem with husbands these days.

WAITER #2. I wake up dead in an airport, working for lousy tips, and you think my biggest problem is lack of trust?

ANGIE. Please don't make a scene, okay?

WAITER #2. Too late for that, after your 'Servingmanophobia' screechfest. *(Takes her hand.)* Look. All that guy sees is the real waiter's face. The one who waited on him before I jumped into this guy's skin suit.

ANGIE. I'm sorry, Snyder. I never meant for this to happen to you. Or to any of them.

WAITER #2. That's what they told me.

ANGIE. You've met the others?

WAITER #2. I got the new corpse initiation right before this body made me finish his shift.

DALE. *(Calling to them.)* Excuse me. Is everything okay?

ANGIE. Great. Fine. Peachy.

WAITER #2. Peachy for you. Post-rigor mortis for me.

DALE. Do you need my help?

ANGIE. No. We're good. We're just talking…um, waiter-y stuff.

WAITER #2. Good save. You should warn him, you know.

ANGIE. I don't think he's interested.

WAITER #2. He'll get there. You remember how much I wasn't interested. Right before I was.

ANGIE. I remember. *(Softens.)* We had good times, didn't we?

WAITER #2. Amazing times. Three months' worth.

ANGIE. I really am sorry, Snyder.

WAITER #2. Yeah. Well, that's life. Or lack of therein. But you should still warn him.

ANGIE. Will it do any good?

WAITER #2. Not at all. But he should know what he's getting himself into.

ANGIE. Snyder…

WAITER #2. I know, Angie. Now go.

> *(She squeezes his hand. A soft moment of loss and regret between them. Then she turns and heads back to Dale's table, as Waiter moves back to the bar, DR.)*

DALE. What was that all about?

ANGIE. Uh, you know. Waiter-y stuff. When to shake. When to stir. He really is fascinating for a restaurant worker.

DALE. A restaurant worker with your dead husband's face.

ANGIE. Did I say that? I meant, um… 'My bed has been replaced.' I uh inventory my furniture when I'm nervous. And then he told me, um… the proper way to open a wine bottle.

DALE. And that is?

ANGIE. That is what?

DALE. The proper way to open a wine bottle?

ANGIE. Oh. Right. Uncork it.

DALE. Glad you got expert advice then.

ANGIE. You can't kiss me, you know.

DALE. I…well…okay…what?

ANGIE. You can't kiss me. Don't even try.

DALE. Who said I was going to kiss you?

ANGIE. That look in your eye. I've seen it before.

DALE. Your late husband?

ANGIE. All of them.

DALE. Exactly how many late husbands do you have?

ANGIE. Counting Snyder? Let me think… there was…. oh, yeah…and then… and how could I forget…Thirteen.

DALE. *(Spits out his drink.)* You have thirteen dead husbands?!

ANGIE. Keep your voice down. He is still pretty sensitive about it.

DALE. Who?

ANGIE. The waiter. Please try to focus on the conversation at hand.

DALE. That's not as easy as it sounds. I'm trying to understand why a waiter…the one you just met and screamed at…would be sensitive about your husband's death?

ANGIE. It's complicated.

DALE. Mega-Understatement there.

ANGIE. In any case, you can't kiss me. It's dangerous.

DALE. I think I get the picture. Herpes?

ANGIE. Ugh, what kind of widow do you think I am?

DALE. I don't know. One with thirteen dead husbands, who screams, then holds hands with strange waiters in an airport lounge at midnight, while her latest honeymoon victim lies dead in a box in Baggage Claim.

ANGIE. Baggage Hold.

DALE. My mistake.

ANGIE. So we both recognize there's this obvious attraction between us. But marriage has to be more than physical attraction.

DALE. Huh? Who said anything about marriage?!

ANGIE. You did. Or you will after you kiss me. You won't be able to help yourself. Neither will I. One second after our lips meet in a soft, sensuous, smoldering kiss, you will suddenly realize that I am the woman of your dreams.

DALE. Sorry, lady, but you are not in my dreams. I dream of faraway lands. Saving humanity. Inventing something brilliant. *(beat.)* Oh, and chickens.

ANGIE. That was before. I am now. Once we kiss, you won't be able to think of anything else. Your whole existence will seem empty and meaningless, if I am not there to share every moment. We will fall madly, passionately in love, and you'll rush out and find the first priest, minister or rabbi who can marry us, and it'll be wonderful and magical. At least for three months, after which you'll die horribly. So best to finish your drink and catch your flight before it is too late.

DALE. *(Pause.)* So back to my earlier question…is there something wrong with you?

ANGIE. Yes. I'm cursed.

DALE. Cursed…but cute. And unlike any woman I have ever met.

ANGIE. See? It's happening already.

DALE. Of course, that could simply mean any woman I met before was normal.

ANGIE. *(Touches his cheek.)* And boring by comparison.

DALE. And boring by comparison.

ANGIE. *(Catches herself, and quickly shoves his face to the side.)* Please run. You have a plane to catch. A life to live, and so many things to accomplish! But only if you leave now.

DALE. *(Rises.)* I have to say; this has been an experience. I'm not exactly sure what kind, but definitely an experience.

ANGIE. Have a nice life, Dale Watterson.

DALE. You too, Angie…Whatever Your Current Last Name Is.

(He picks up his coat. And heads off UR. Waiter #2 leaning over the bar begins to count to on his fingers. Before he reaches five, Dale turns back around.)

DALE. You know, it's funny. I never gave the slightest thought to kissing you, until…

ANGIE. Sorry I brought it up. Have a good flight.

DALE. …now I can't seem to get your lips out of my mind…

ANGIE. Play Sudoku on the plane. That should help.

DALE. Would it really be soft, sensuous and smoldering?

ANGIE. And dangerous. Don't forget dangerous.

DALE. But free of Herpes?

ANGIE. Hundred-percent Herpes-free. Far more lethal.

LOUDSPEAKER VOICE. Flight 359 to Nashville…Now Boarding at Gate B-19.

ANGIE: Isn't that your flight?

DALE. Right. Goodbye, Angie Buckner.

ANGIE. Goodbye, Dale Waterson.

(They share a moment of quiet longing. Until Dale slinks off, UR. Angie slumps. Waiter #2 crosses to her table bearing two drinks.)

WAITER #2. Drink this.

ANGIE. What is it?

WAITER #2. Does it matter?

(She looks up at him with sorrow. Then downs the drink in one gulp.)

ANGIE. That was close.

WAITER #2. You did the right thing.

ANGIE. I'll tell myself that when I'm lying in bed alone for the next thirty or forty years.

WAITER #2. We both know that ain't gonna happen.

(He hands her the second drink. She downs that too.)

WAITER #2. I'll leave you alone.

ANGIE. For now.

(The Waiter exits, DL. Angie sighs. Gathers up her purse and starts to slump off towards Baggage Claim. That is, until Dale returns. Wide-eyed and breathless.)

DALE. Angie…

ANGIE. Dale!

(She brightens. Then the realization hits her, and she tries to turn away. But he pulls her into a passionate embrace. They stare longingly into each other's eyes, before he bends into a kiss. Soft, sensuous and smoldering. STAGE LIGHTS PULSE & CHANGE COLOR around them as they kiss. They are both breathless when they come up for air.)

DALE. You…you ARE the woman of my dreams!

ANGIE. *(Sadly.)* That's what they all say.

(As they kiss once more, the lights around them SLOWLY DIM, except a single reddish yellow spot that leaves them frozen in mid-kiss.)

END OF ACT ONE, SCENE 1

ACT ONE
Scene 2

AT RISE: The stage is in darkness, except a single red spotlight Downstage Right, in which Angie and Dale remain frozen in mid-kiss.

(Our NARRATOR steps from the shadows, into his own yellow spot, Stage Left. He looks at the kissing couple trapped in the only other circle of light on stage.)

NARRATOR. There are some kisses we always remember. Our first real kiss, where the warmth and wonder of youth meets the nervous yearning of looming adulthood. When we suddenly discover that our desperate Disney dreams have come true, and that someone, somehow sees us as someone worth having.

(He watches as Dale & Angie's spotlight slowly, almost imperceptibly pales. In the shadows behind them, the STAGE HANDS quietly remove the signs, tables and traces of the Airport Lounge, and begin to transform the space into a well-appointed living room.)

NARRATOR. Then there is the very first kiss with the love of our life. When tender trembling lips know, even before our heart does, that despite billions of people in the world, and the astronomical odds, our soulmate - the one we have waited for all these years - has finally found us. And finally transformed our isolated identity into the joyous embrace of two-person *'us-ness.'* Lips first, we become whole. As that most gentle of personal touches breathes purpose into our soaring, celebrating soul.

(The spotlight on Dale and Angie has completed its journey to a sterile whitish blue. Their frozen forms have yet to notice, even though a tinge of sadness has colored the Narrator's voice.)

The Kiss Me Curse

NARRATOR. Finally, there is the last kiss we share with the one we believed really was the love of our life. Warm lips betray an increasingly cold heart. And in that once joyous act, we suddenly find that something so comforting, so life-sustaining, has slipped away, leaving more memory than emotion in the sadly silent scream of its absence…

> *(Angie breaks the freeze, staring long and regretfully at a confused Dale, before she slips off UL. Leaving him alone in the cold blue circle of light.)*

NARRATOR. That is the saddest kiss of all. One we realize only in hindsight. A poignant phrase of poetic passion that was never supposed to end…

> *(The spots fade as stage lights come up around our Narrator and the lost and wondering Dale.)*

DALE. Angie?

> *(The illumination reveals we are now in an upscale apartment. A fireplace adorns the Upstage Center wall, with a large framed portrait of Dale and Angie above the mantel. A sofa dominates Center Stage, with end tables framing its place in the room.)*

NARRATOR. But end it does. And this is where we resume our story…

> *(Dale wanders around, as if seeing the space for the very first time. With one last look of pity toward the increasingly desperate Dale, our Narrator exits DL.)*

DALE. Where did you go, Angie?

> *(Dale dashes off, UR. After a beat, Angie enters through a door UL. She wears a tight black dress. Looks up at the portrait of her and Dale, before pulling it down off the wall.)*

DALE. *(Entering.)* What are you doing?

ANGIE. Aaaaaahhh!

DALE. No need to scream. There aren't any waiters here.

ANGIE. You scared me!

DALE. Not exactly the reaction a newlywed is looking for. You want to tell me why you are taking the picture of us down?

ANGIE. It's too painful. It hurts me to look at it.

DALE. How do you think I feel?

ANGIE. I don't know. Awful, I guess.

DALE. What happened to us, Angie?

ANGIE. What we always knew would happen.

DALE. I didn't know it would happen. Things were great. Amazing. Wonderful. The best three months of my life! Then suddenly I look around and you're gone. You don't leave a note. Don't say goodbye. Don't give me any idea when you'll be back.

ANGIE. Oh, God. You don't know, do you?

DALE. Know what? That you sneak out and leave me here alone? That you show up wearing a sexy black dress and taking our picture down from the wall. There's someone else, isn't there?

ANGIE. No. At least not yet.

DALE. What's that supposed to mean?!

ANGIE. I love you, Dale. More than I should have. But we're not us anymore. I warned you this would happen.

DALE. Stop saying that! You stood at an altar three months ago and promised 'til death do us part.'

ANGIE. And I kept that vow, sweetheart…

DALE. Liar.

(Snyder/Waiter #2 enters, DR.)

SNYDER. She's telling the truth, buddy.

DALE. Who the hell are you? What are you doing in our apartment?

SNYDER. First of all, this isn't your apartment. I helped pay for it. Me and the others.

DALE. What others? Is this the guy you've been seeing?

ANGIE. Every day for the last six months.

DALE. Tramp.

SNYDER. Don't you talk to my wife that way!

DALE. Your wife?! *(To Angie.)* What are you? A bigamist?!

SNYDER. Not too bright, is he?

ANGIE. Come on, Snyder. You remember how difficult this can be.

DALE. Angie, who is this guy?

ANGIE. Snyder. The guy I told you about when we met in the airport.

DALE. Your last husband? You said he was dead.

SNYDER. Bingo.

DALE. You expect me to believe he's some kind of ghost or something?

SNYDER. We prefer the term Ethereal-American. Why don't you ask your wife where she's been?

DALE. Where have you been, Angie?

ANGIE. *(Softly.)* I was burying my husband.

SNYDER. Tell him how it felt.

ANGIE. Familiar. Way too familiar.

DALE. What kind of game are you two playing?

SNYDER. Open your eyes, Sherlock. Your wife is in a black dress. She's taking down your portrait because it's too painful for her. You can see her dead ex-husband. She just came back from a funeral. So if we put that all together, it means…

DALE. I'm dead? *(Stunned.)* I can't be dead. I'm standing here looking at both of you.

SNYDER. Your widow and her dead husband.

DALE. *(Sudden realization.)* The Kiss Me Curse. It's been three months. Three months since we first kissed…

SNYDER. He may have zero brain waves, but he's not as dumb as he looks.

ANGIE. Be nice, Snyder.

SNYDER. Why should I? I've watched him sleeping with my wife for the last three months.

ANGIE. He's been sleeping with his wife. Your widow. Now his widow too.

DALE. I'm dead? How did I die?

ANGIE. Artistically.

DALE. I think it's coming back to me. Was I in the shower?

ANGIE. Yes.

(Dale collapses on the sofa.)

DALE. Uh oh. I know where this is going…

ANGIE. Most people sing in the shower. How did I know you like to dance in there?

DALE. I can't help it. I dance when I'm happy.

ANGIE. Note to self…Don't make them happy in the shower.

SNYDER. Nice to meet ya, Happy Feet.

DALE. Don't call me that.

SNYDER. Okay, Slick.

DALE. I don't like that either.

ANGIE. Ease up on him, Snyder. You remember how hard first recognition can be.

DALE. First recognition?

SNYDER. She means when you first realize you're dead. Deceased. Laid out. Ex humanus.

ANGIE. Snyder, please…

SNYDER. The big sleep. Worm food. Pushing up daisies.

ANGIE. Snyder…

SNYDER. Bought the farm. Kicked the bucket. Took a dirt nap. Assumed room temperature.

ANGIE. Cut it out!

SNYDER. *(Shrugs.)* Just tryin' to help.

DALE. I can't believe I'm dead… Ever since I was a kid, I was never afraid of dying. I…I just didn't want to die stupid.

SNYDER. Guess you didn't reach that lofty goal, did ya, Happy Feet?

ANGIE. Enough!

SNYDER. I can't help it. The image of you doing a slip and slide somersault in the shower is burned into our retinas. Or it would be, if we still had retinas. Or eyeballs. Or any physical stuff at all.

DALE. You keep saying 'we.'

SNYDER. The other twelve Angie exes. Counting me, you are number fourteen.

DALE. *(Rising.)* How could you do this to me, Angie?

ANGIE. I warned you not to kiss me.

DALE. I was in love. Who listens to warnings? I was swept away by your eyes. Your smile. Your warm, touch. Your…

ANGIE. Please don't do that.

DALE. Do what?

ANGIE. Fall in love with me again. It's extremely impolite after you're dead.

DALE. Impolite?

ANGIE. Not to mention impractical. Better if you just hang back with the boys and take the spectator seats.

DALE. The boys?

(JARED enters, UL. Just 18. Tall, lanky and clueless. He looks like he walked out of a 1990's Teen Beat magazine.)

JARED. This the new guy? Welcome to 'Afterlife with Angie.'

DALE. Who are you?

JARED. Husband Number Primo. Angie's initial ex. I like, started the whole ball rolling, metaphysically speaking.

DALE. I'm dead. I'm really dead…

SNYDER. Welcome to our world, Slick.

DALE. *(To Angie.)* Did you ever love me?

ANGIE. Oh, Dale…of course I did1 Once our lips met, I fell just as hard as you did. It's part of the curse.

DALE. You haven't shed a single tear for me.

JARED. She can't, man. Her teardrops have been like, I dunno, 'spelled' shut or something.

SNYDER. It's part of the curse. Maybe the cruelest part. She falls in love but can't cry a single tear when she loses us.

JARED. Way harsh, dude.

DALE. Harsh? At least she didn't die.

ANGIE. Part of me did. Part of me always does. Imagine what it's like to fall deeply and completely in love over and over again, only to go to funeral after funeral. Losing the loves of my life as soon as I find them.

SNYDER. And think of what it's like for the rest of us. We may be dead, but we still love her. And we have to stand helplessly by, watching her suffer the same loss, time and time again.

ANGIE. Believe me, Dale. If I could change places with you, I would. But Snyder and the others won't let me end the curse.

JARED. Not if it means killing yourself.

ANGIE. I don't know of any other way to stop it! I even hid out at a convent in Spain for six months…up until Brother Padrigo came to visit.

DALE. Brother Padrigo?

SNYDER. A monk. Husband Number eight.

JARED. Cool dude. Still racked by the guilt thing though.

SNYDER. But I have to admit, the man can chant.

JARED. Righteously.

DALE. Let me get this straight…you seduced a monk?!

ANGIE. I wasn't trying to. It's the curse.

DALE. But still, seducing a monk? It's not like you get an 'oopsy' pass for not trying that hard!

SNYDER. Ease up, Twinkle Toes.

DALE. Sorry if I don't have much sympathy for Brother Padrigo, or any of the rest of you. I'm still trying to absorb the concept of my own demise. I had so many plans. So many dreams…

SNYDER. So many pliés. So many disco moves left to try.

ANGIE. Snyder!

SNYDER. Hey, death by dancing is considered a preferred way to go with this curse.

JARED. Seriously. Much better than Hubby Number Six.

ANGIE. Poor Bernard.

DALE. What happened to Bernard?

JARED. Death by sneezing.

DALE. That doesn't sound so bad.

SNYDER. It wasn't the 'how' as much as the 'where.'

JARED. Check this out. Three months to the day after, you know, his first kiss, the dude was in a public restroom…

SNYDER. …when he started to sniffle.

DALE. How is that tragic?

ANGIE. Bernard had a really hefty sneeze.

JARED. Dude sneezed so hard, he knocked himself out on the urinal. They found him lying on the floor with the front of his skull caved in.

SNYDER. *(Chuckling.)* With his embarrassment hanging out there for everyone to see.

JARED. *(Laughing.)* Awesome fail, man!

ANGIE. It wasn't funny.

SNYDER. Sure it was. The rest of us exes still tease him about his dangling participle. And now that you've joined the Brotherhood of Dead Husbands, you get to tease him too.

DALE. Can't I just move on? I mean, isn't there a heaven or nirvana or something where we end up?

JARED. Hard to tell. We're stuck here as long as the curse holds. After that, like, who knows? Major mystery time.

DALE. *(To Angie.)* Well, since I'm already dead, can I kiss you again?

ANGIE. I wish you could, Dale.

SNYDER. You are nothing but energy now. All habeas. No corpus.

DALE. But I feel real. *(Thumps his chest.)* See?

SNYDER. Sorry, Tarzan. You may feel like you have a body, but you're nothing more than vapor with memories.

JARED. It kinda takes some getting used to.

DALE. I don't believe you guys.

SNYDER. Then go ahead. Try to kiss her.

(Dale moves toward Angie, lips puckered with determination. Two feet from her, he stops, as if hitting an invisible wall. Try as he might, he cannot move closer, remains stuck in place.)

DALE. I can't move! Why can't I move?

SNYDER. You're playing by afterlife rules now.

JARED. Yeah, like lip limbo with the living is no-no number one.

(Dale struggles to move. Angie can't bear to see him struggle. She collapses on the floor.)

ANGIE. Oh, Dale…

DALE. Angie…?

SNYDER. Stand down, Romeo! Can't you see what this is doing to her? She loves us. Each of us. Seeing us struggle just makes it worse.

DALE. I…I'm sorry, Angie. I just wanted you to know how much I love you.

SNYDER. She knows, stupid. And seeing us reminds her of it and drives the pain home even more. What's worse, only Angie can see or hear us. It's another vicious part of the curse. All designed to drive her crazy.

ANGIE. *(Weakly.)* I'm sorry, Dale… I'm so sorry…

DALE. It kills me to see her likes this.

JARED. Kills all of us, man.

SNYDER. And it kills her to know she killed us. *(Sadly.)* Let's give our girl some 'alone time.' She needs privacy to grieve over you.

JARED. Come on, Newly-dead Dude. I'll introduce you to the others.

DALE. *(Softening.)* Will she be okay?

JARED. No.

SNYDER. She never will be…

> *(The three late husbands stare at the broken woman, before sadly slinking off, UR.)*

END OF ACT ONE, SCENE 2

ACT ONE
Scene 3

AT RISE: Narrator enters, DL. Gestures to the broken hearted Angie still crumpled on the floor.)

NARRATOR. Sad, isn't it? Some of you might not have expected such heartrending emotions in a comedy. But to be fair, we did put the word 'Curse' in the title. And curses are seldom cheerful or cuddly affairs. *(Sighs.)* So here we have Angie, destined to repeat a pattern of love and loss for the rest of her life.

For those of you who weren't paying attention, here are the details of the 'Kiss Me' Curse. Men meet Angie and soon develop an overwhelming urge to kiss her. Once their lips meet, both the 'kisser' and the 'kissee' fall madly in love. It always ends in tragedy.

Those of you who came in with a spouse, might want to grab your husband's arm to keep him in his seat. I can see this guy in the fourth row eyeing Angie and thinking that it may be worth it. Behave yourself, sir!

As I was saying, the 'kisser' and the 'kissee' fall passionately in love and feel an irresistible need to get married. They are deliriously happy together, as only Hollywood and fictional plays can portray love. But exactly three months after that first kiss, the new husband dies a tragic and often embarrassing death. To make matters worse, the ghosts of Angie's dead exes are doomed to hover around her forever, so she feels even more wretched for shattering so many lives.

(STAGE HANDS start removing the furnishings and set pieces of Angie's apartment. They wheel in two façades of lockers, hang hand painted signs that reads "Go Pewee Valley Fighting Poodles!" and "Order your prom tickets today!"

NARRATOR. You might ask "Who would place such a terrible curse on such a nice young woman?" For that, we must go back a number of years to Angie's senior year at Pewee Valley High.

(A Stage Hand walks over to the still sniffling Angie and hands her a backpack and a high school letter jacket, as she wraps her hair in a ponytail.)

NARRATOR. Ahh, high school. That savage and wonderful time when acne, hormones and insecurities run rampant. When kids are cruel, being popular matters more than breathing, and absolutely everything is so amazingly, awesomely, astoundingly important you could just die! At least it feels that way at the time. Just ask Angie.

(Angie still sniffles in what is now our high school setting. She tries to hide her tears, as JARED DIMWITTY enters, UR. Jared is tall, gaunt and brooding, with that casually bored Bad Boy look that is irresistible to high school girls.)

JARED. Yo. What's with the face, Angie? You're like, crying.

ANGIE. No, I'm not.

JARED. Then like, your eyes are leaking. A lot.

ANGIE. I can't fool you, Jared. You're way smart.

JARED. It's a curse. I wanted to be cool from birth, but I got stuck with all this oversized brain matter instead. So like, what's with all of that dreary-osity?

ANGIE. Nothing.

JARED. It can't be nothing. I think it's something, and like, I'm way smart, remember?

ANGIE. I'm just sad, I guess. Prom is coming up, and Billy and I broke up last week. I doubt anyone will ask me to Prom now.

JARED. Prom drama. I get it. It's a chick thing, right?

ANGIE. I guess. I don't want to be one of *those* girls. The ones everyone feels sorry for because they missed out on their Senior Prom. People remember things like that…for like, centuries!

JARED. Yeah. Scarred for life. But hey, you're not all that abominable. You've got it going on in the face department. Most dudes would jump at the chance to pull you right out of the sad girl ghetto.

ANGIE. Aw, Jared. You say the sweetest things.

JARED. Yeah. 'Cuz of my majorly large brain and all. But hey, like, if I wasn't going with Maggie Sagworth…

ANGIE. But you are.

JARED. But, yeah, like, if I wasn't…

ANGIE. But you are.

JARED. I know. But I mean, like, if I was a free agent type, and basically un-prommed at this particular moment in time…

ANGIE. You mean…if you weren't going steady with Maggie?

JARED. Or if maybe she had like, a sudden brain aneurism that affected her left leg and she couldn't dance right, y'know?

ANGIE. Then she couldn't go to Prom.

JARED. Like, no way. I mean, I wouldn't embarrass her like that with all those seriously ugly aneuristic leg spasms and all.

ANGIE. You are way too nice to take a girl with seriously ugly aneuristic leg spasms to the Prom.

JARED. So like, if something like that happened, tragic as it may be, I'd be tempted to y'know, ask you.

ANGIE. You would, Jared? You would ask me to the Prom?

JARED. Only if like she had a major short circuit in her frontal lobes, y'know?

ANGIE. But Maggie doesn't have a short circuit in her frontal lobes. *(Sighs.)* She doesn't have anything like that.

JARED. Yeah. I mean no. At least I don't think so.

ANGIE. So you have to take her to the Prom.

JARED. Yeah… I mean like, yeah.

ANGIE. Maggie sure is lucky. She has a perfectly normal brain, non-spasmodic legs, and a boyfriend as awesome as you. I bet she's even a better kisser than me.

JARED. I don't know nothin' about that. I mean… Like, I never even kissed you or anything yet.

ANGIE. You probably wouldn't want to. You're probably used to Maggie's tired old chapped lips. How long have you been going out now?

JARED. *(Counts on his fingers.)* Five months, I think.

ANGIE. Five months! That's practically *forever* in school years. You guys are like an old married couple!

JARED. I am? I mean, we are?

ANGIE. Completely. Locked in for life. Kissing a fresh pair of lips would be so… wrong.

JARED. Yeah…like, so wrong.

ANGIE. Wouldn't it?

JARED. I guess. Like, I guess.

ANGIE. *(Putting on fresh Chapstick.)* So I better keep my lips to myself… I wouldn't want you thinking about my soft, warm, cherry-flavored lips when you're kissing Maggie's tired old…

(Jared grabs her and kisses her. She does not resist. Suddenly, MAGGIE SAGWORTH enters, DL. A dark-haired teenager dressed all in black, with a slightly mysterious look.)

MAGGIE. Jared!!

(Angie and Jared leap apart.)

MAGGIE. What are you doing?!

JARED. Nothing, Maggie. I was just…um, nothing.

MAGGIE. You were kissing Angie!

JARED. Naw, I was just like… consoling her.

MAGGIE. With your mouth?! Was this tramp trying to get you to dump me and take her to the Prom?

ANGIE. Who are you calling a tramp?!

MAGGIE. If the lip fits…

JARED. Whoa! Prom drama. Way too heavy for me.

MAGGIE. *(Grabbing Jared's shirt.)* You tried to steal my boyfriend!

ANGIE. Jared's a big boy. He can make up his own mind. *(Also yanking his shirt.)* So who's the better kisser, Jared?

MAGGIE. Yeah, who?

JARED. Well, like, from a purely science-type comparison…

MAGGIE. Yeah?

JARED. I'd have to go with Angie. The girl's got some serious lip talent.

MAGGIE. So you're dumping me?

JARED. Dumping is so harsh a verbiage. I'm like, setting you free. And if I come back someday, it was like, meant to be. Otherwise, probably nah unh, y'know?

MAGGIE. You think her kiss is so irresistible? Then, so be it!

JARED. So be what?

(MAGGIE's face darkens, as do the stage lights around her as she begins a deep throated CHANT.)

MAGGIE. Harstel Forgam Selkilat Gort…

(STAGE LIGHTS FLICKER RED as she raises her arms. Jared and Angie recoil in fear.)

MAGGIE. Beluman Groozel Kislefreg Panukum Verg!

ANGIE. What's happening?!

JARED. I dunno. But it ain't good!

MAGGIE. Harble Harren Harrara Hazzelllika HAHDZAAALL!!

THE KISS ME CURSE

(SUDDEN BLACKOUT. A CRASH OF THUNDER. A SCREAM in the darkness, followed by a long silence. When the lights finally come back up, the three of them are standing there, just like before.)

JARED. That was…like…y'know, way anti-climactic.

ANGIE. What did you do, Maggie?

MAGGIE. Something my Great Aunt Tessruda taught me.

ANGIE. Gibberish?

MAGGIE. You'll see.

ANGIE. See what?

MAGGIE. You'll see what you'll see. When it's time to see it.

ANGIE. Is that supposed to creep me out?

MAGGIE. Why should it? You're evidently the better kisser. And you obviously have no problem making brain-dead men fall all over you.

JARED. Hey, like… hey!

MAGGIE. So since kissing is your gift, I merely amped up the volume a bit. Then added a few consequences.

ANGIE. What do you mean 'amped up the volume?' What kind of consequences?

MAGGIE. You'll see. In exactly three months. *(Starts to walk off.)* Enjoy the Prom, you two. *(Sadly.)* I'm sure you'll have the time of your life, Jared.

(A tender moment, then she smacks his arm and exits DL.)

ANGIE. Ooooh! That Maggie is soooo uncool.

JARED. *(A confused pause, then…)* Kiss me.

ANGIE. What?

JARED. Kiss me. Y'know, with those lips of yours.

ANGIE. *(Shrugs.)* Okay.

(Angie takes out her chewing gum and kisses him. They both become swept away as the STAGE LIGHTS FLICKER around them. They break apart, breathless.)

ANGIE.   That was weird. Really wow, but weird.

JARED.   Let's get married.

ANGIE.   What?

(Jared grabs Angie's hand and excitedly pulls her off, UR. Narrator enters DL.)

NARRATOR.   They say 'Hell hath no fury like a woman scorned.' That's twice as true when Prom is involved. As Maggie said, Jared did have the time of his life. A life which ended exactly three months later, when the self-proclaimed boy genius tried to use a blow dryer in the shower. The resulting sparks blacked out two city blocks, and it took a month to get the smell of seared meat out of Angie's new apartment.

(STAGE HANDS take down the lockers and high school set.)

NARRATOR.   The police originally wanted to charge Angie with murder, figuring nobody would be stupid enough to use an electrical device in the shower. But once they spoke to anyone who knew Jared…they let her go. And so the curse began.

(The STAGE HANDS pull a thin carpet of artificial grass across the stage, with a row of tombstones attached to it.)

NARRATOR.   And so, a simple indiscretion by a lonely teenager began a never-ending cycle of love and heartbreak. Popular kids wonder, "Is there life after high school?' In Angie's case, there was only sadness. And death…

(Angie enters, and stands before the tombstones, looking mournful. Although Angie is back to present day, Jared enters and stands behind the tombstones, still looking high school age.)

JARED.   Yo, Angie. Thanks for visiting.

ANGIE.   Of course, Jared. I'm sorry I put you here.

JARED.   It's cool. How did I die again?

ANGIE. Stupidly.

JARED. But what about my massively sized brain?

ANGIE. An autopsy revealed that might have been a bit of an exaggeration.

JARED. Huh?

(Snyder Enters. Stands behind his own tombstone.)

SNYDER. They said you were a moron.

JARED. Hey, like…hey!

ANGIE. Be nice, Snyder.

SNYDER. Nice? This guy barbecues himself in the shower and nearly gets you arrested. And I'm supposed to be nice with him? What did you ever see in this Kentucky Fried Idiot anyways?

ANGIE. He was my first.

SNYDER. Your first husband? Your first victim? Your first…

JARED. Like, all of the above, man.

SNYDER. *(Muttering.)* Must have been some curse…

JARED. You should talk, 'Mr. Died-Doing-The-Dirty.' At least I died washing up instead of….

(Dale enters. Moves behind his tombstone.)

DALE. Will you two keep it down? All this noise could wake the dead.

JARED. That's like, a joke, right?

DALE. Duh, yeah. It's like a joke. *(Shakes his head.)* Must have been some curse.

SNYDER. That's what I said.

ANGIE. Come on, boys. No need to fight. I loved each one of you, and still do. It breaks my heart to see you fighting.

SNYDER. What do you expect? You were the love of my life.

JARED. All our lives.

DALE. And still are.

SNYDER. Even though we're dead, it doesn't make sharing you any easier.

ANGIE. I know. Believe me, I know. My heart is sliced into fourteen equal pieces.

SNYDER. It's tough to think one of those equal pieces belongs to Muffy Einstein here.

JARED. Hey, like…hey!

SNYDER. Snappy comeback.

DALE. Uh oh. Potential ex-husband at four o'clock. Better run, Angie.

SNYDER. Too late. He's seen her.

DALE. Be rude to him, Angie.

JARED. Like, Ultra-rude.

ANGIE. I'll try.

(WADDY enters. 40. Bad suit. Cheesy smile. He holds a bunch of flowers.)

WADDY. You all right, little lady?

SNYDER. Starting off with a diminutive. Always a classy move.

DALE. For a cave man.

WADDY. Don't mean to disrupt your melancholy, but you sure look like you've seen a ghost.

ANGIE. You have no idea.

JARED. Be rude, Angie. Mega rude.

ANGIE. I will.

WADDY. You will, what?

ANGIE. I will…um, appreciate it if you leave me to mourn my husband in peace.

WADDY. Sure thing. Which one is your husband?

ANGIE. The first two rows.

WADDY. Huh?

ANGIE. Look, you seem like a nice guy, Mr…..

WADDY. Waddy.

SNYDER. Waddy?

ANGIE. Waddy?

WADDY. Waddy Peytona. Fertilizer King of the Midwest.

ANGIE. I thought I sensed a stench of royalty about you.

WADDY. Good one. But I'll have you know that fertilizer is America's greatest natural resource.

SNYDER. Bullshit.

ANGIE. Bullshit.

WADDY. That there would be the organic variety. I'll have you know fertilizer is more valuable than gold. You can't grow food in gold flakes. It takes animal droppings.

ANGIE. Lovely.

DALE. Please tell me I'm not dead and listening to a lecture on fertilizer.

SNYDER. Death ain't all it's cracked up to be, is it, Happy Feet?

WADDY. It's true! The Great Plains only became America's breadbasket after a few billion buffalo crapped all over it for centuries. Waste not, taste not, I always say. *(Pulls a candy bar out of his pocket.)* Chocolate?

ANGIE. Uh…

WADDY. Heh heh. A little joke of mine. Actually, less of a joke than a humorous juxtaposition, considering the topic we were discussing.

ANGIE. Funny.

WADDY. I even had my name printed on the label. *(Shows her the candy bar.)* See?

ANGIE. *(Reading.)* "Waddy Peytona. The Fertilizer King. You'll flip for my chips."

WADDY. Clever, huh?

SNYDER. Can you believe this guy?

ANGIE. I'm speechless.

WADDY. Makes a great sales tool. And it really cracks up the gang down at Manure University. That's our industry training camp. Sure I can't interest you?

ANGIE. Fertilizer-themed chocolate? I'll pass.

WADDY. Good one. So what's a pretty lady like you doing in a place like this?

ANGIE. Mourning…Dead husbands…Remember?

JARED. And they say I'm dumb!

SNYDER. They don't just say it. They wrote it on your tombstone.

JARED. Hey, like… *(Looks at his tombstone.)* Hey!

ANGIE. Look, Mr. Fertilizer King…

WADDY. Call me Waddy. No need to use the Royal We.

ANGIE. Waddy. I appreciate the PBS special on organic nutrients…but if you know what's good for you, you'll hit the road. Take off running and never look back.

WADDY. I get the distinct impression you don't want me here.

JARED. Ha! *(Looks at the others.)* Don't say it.

ANGIE. I'm only thinking of you, so that I don't ever have to be thinking of you.

WADDY. Well, at least you're thinking of me. *(Hands her the flowers.)* Pretty flowers for a pretty lady.

ANGIE. Uh, didn't you bring them for someone else?

WADDY. *(Shrugs.)* They're dead. They won't miss 'em.

SNYDER. Oh, sure. Dis the deceased!

DALE. I don't like this guy.

JARED. Me either. He don't seem that bright to me. *(Notices the other ghosts staring at him.)* What?

ANGIE. What?

WADDY. What, what?

ANGIE. What…ever you do, don't kiss me, okay?

WADDY. I wasn't plannin' on it…at least 'til you mentioned it. Now that's about all I can think of…

JARED. Damn, it's happening again.

ANGIE. Damn, it's happening again.

WADDY. What's happening?

ANGIE. Nothing. Please go away.

WADDY. You ain't got that tight a grip on reality, do ya, little lady?

DALE. I so don't like this guy!

SNYDER. It'd be worth kissing him just to stop him from saying 'little lady' again.

ANGIE. *(To exes.)* Stop that.

WADDY. Stop what?

ANGIE. Stop…uh, looking at me like that…

(Their eyes meet. Linger.)

JARED. Uh oh.

SNYDER. Curse time.

JARED. Majorly.

DALE. You mean, we may have to share eternity with the Fertilizer King?

SNYDER. Looks like it.

WADDY. I really need to kiss you.

ANGIE. I know. But you really shouldn't.

WADDY. I didn't get to be the Fertilizer King by doing things I should've.

JARED. What's THAT supposed to mean?

SNYDER. I don't want to know.

ANGIE. Please go away. Please...?

WADDY. Say it again.

ANGIE. Say what?

WADDY. Please.

ANGIE. *(Breathless. Drawn to his lips.)* ...please...?

> *(STAGE LIGHTS FLICKER as he kisses her. She responds with curse-enhanced enthusiasm. The exes cringe behind their tombstones.)*

ANGIE. *(Dreamily.)* Hmmm. Tastes like chocolate.

DALE. At least there's that.

WADDY. Wow. I ain't never been kissed like that before!

SNYDER. Looks like our Angie's falling again.

JARED. Poor Angie.

DALE. Poor us.

SNYDER. Let's give them some privacy, boys.

> *(Angie & Waddy kiss again, as the ghosts file off-stage.)*

DALE. I sure hope this cemetery offers a Frequent Die-er Discount.

CURTAIN

End of Act One, Scene 3

ACT ONE
Scene 4

AT RISE: *Lights remain out, as the stage is once again in Angie's apartment, only now a large bed sits Center Stage, with the sofa moved UL.*

We hear a MOAN and a THUD in the darkness.

A FLASHLIGHT clicks on. The only light on stage. Waddy, in bed with Angie, shines the light on her sleeping face. At this point, the flashlight is the only light on stage.)

WADDY.   Angie. Angie, darling! Wake up!

ANGIE.   Mmmnnnph….

WADDY.   Angie! Are you okay?

ANGIE.   Huh? Wha…?

WADDY.   You fainted. Or passed out or something.

ANGIE.   Passed out…?

WADDY.   Yeah. We were…being romantic. Then your eyes rolled back in your head and you fainted. Scared me to death.

ANGIE.   Scared you…? I…

   (She sits up in bed. Looks at him and SCREAMS. So does he.)

ANGIE.   Aaaaaaaarrgh!

WADDY.   Aaaaaaaarrgh! Wait…what are we screaming for?

ANGIE.   *(Grabbing the flashlight and shining it in his face.)* You! Me! How long have I been out?

WADDY.   I don't know. Four or five minutes. What happened?

ANGIE. Four or five minutes? That's too soon! It's getting faster.

WADDY. What's getting faster?

ANGIE. The curse.

WADDY. Not that again. I told you it's all in your head.

ANGIE. Yeah? Then look over there.

WADDY. Where?

ANGIE. *(Points the flashlight.)* Behind the sofa. Then you go and tell me it's all in my head.

> *(Waddy climbs out of the bed. He is wearing only a white tank top and a ridiculous pair of heart strewn underwear. Angie's flashlight lands on a pair of bare legs on the floor peeking out from behind the sofa.)*

WADDY. Aaaaaaaaaargh! Who is that?!

> *(The body wears matching heart shaped boxer shorts. The upper torso covered by a white sheet.)*

ANGIE. Don't you recognize those legs? That underwear? The birthmark on his...

WADDY. Aaaaaaaargh!

> *(Angie flicks on a light switch and the stage is bathed in light. Over the mantel is the same portrait of Angie and her husband, only now Dale's face has been replaced by Waddy's.*
>
> *And on the floor behind the sofa...)*

WADDY. That's me!

ANGIE. Uh huh.

WADDY. How can that be me? I'm me!

> *(Snyder enters from DR.)*

SNYDER. You were you, buddy. Now you're just an ice cold meatloaf with bad taste in underwear.

WADDY. Aaaaaaaaaargh!

SNYDER. Screams a lot, doesn't he?

WADDY. Who are you?!

SNYDER. Number Thirteen on Angie's Hit Parade. Call me Snyder.

WADDY. What are you doing here? And what am I doing *there?!*

SNYDER. You want the good news or the bad news? The bad news is you're dead. Deceased. Ex humanus. Worm food....

ANGIE. Snyder...

SNYDER. How ya doing, babe?

> *(Angie lifts the covers as Snyder climbs into bed beside her. Waddy still stares at the body in confusion.)*

WADDY. What's the good news?

SNYDER. Well, Fertilizer Boy. Even dead, you couldn't possibly smell any worse.

WADDY. Are you kidding?

> *(Jared enters, UL.)*

JARED. No, dude. There's an aftersmell that followed you into the afterlife. Seriously odiferous, man.

WADDY. Aaaaargh! Who's he?

ANGIE. That's Jared. Guys, please give him a break.

JARED. You know how they say, 'You can't take it with you?' That should have included your odor. *(To Snyder.)* Scoot your bod over, man.

> *(Angie raises the covers again and Jared squeezes into bed with them. Dale enters UR. He stops, waves his hand and grimaces.)*

DALE. Ugh. What is...that?!

SNYDER. Manure Man just joined our ice-cold entourage.

DALE. Seriously? I have no living nostrils, but have to put up with that for eternity?

WADDY. *(Collapses onto the sofa.)* This can't be happening. I can't be dead. I have deals to make. Bills to pay…

DALE. Showers to take.

SNYDER. Speaking of showers…

DALE. Don't say it!

WADDY. I always thought I'd do something important in my life. Maybe even have a freeway exit named after me. Not just be remembered for embodying the sweet smell of success…

(The guys choke, snort and laugh.)

WADDY. It's an expression!

ANGIE. Boys…

(Dale climbs in Angie's side of the bed.)

DALE. Sorry, sweetheart. With all these ex-husbands, you gotta get a bigger bed.

(Waddy reaches down and pokes the dead legs by the couch.)

WADDY. I can't feel my legs.

SNYDER. If it's any consolation, they can't feel you either.

ANGIE. I can't believe it! The curse is speeding up. It used to be weeks after you guys died before I would see you. Then days and hours. Now it's less than five minutes!

JARED. Premature ghostification. It happens, dude.

ANGIE. I don't think I can take this anymore…

SNYDER. There, there, sweetheart. It's okay.

DALE. We're here for you.

JARED. All of us.

(The three console Angie, as she sits up in bed.)

WADDY. Hey, do you mind? My body's still warm. Get the hell out of my bed!

SNYDER. You don't like it; you shouldn't have gone for the gold medal in contortionism.

WADDY. Contortionism? What are you talking about?

JARED. How you died, dude. It was gnarly.

DALE. But rather impressive.

WADDY. Wait, how did I die?

SNYDER. With a bang.

WADDY. Huh?

ANGIE. Do you remember that new position you wanted to try? Page One-thirteen in the Karma Sutra?

WADDY. Yeah.

ANGIE. It wasn't a good idea.

DALE. You lost your balance and did a swan dive off the bed.

SNYDER. Landed face first. Your neck snapped so loud; we could hear it in the afterlife.

WADDY. You were watching?

SNYDER. Hey, we're dead. There's not a lot we get to do on the other side.

JARED. Like not even basic cable, dude. So we binge-watched your honeymoon.

WADDY. Really? *(Beat.)* How was it?

SNYDER. No plot, but the action scenes were rather interesting.

DALE. Could have done without the soundtrack, though.

JARED. Yeah, dude. You grunt like a Neambutol.

DALE. Neanderthal. *(Pronounced with a th.)*

ANGIE. It's Neanderthal. *(Pronounced with a hard t sound.)*

(The four in bed start arguing. "Are you sure?" "I don't think so." "I've never heard that before." etc.)

JARED. Whatever! We all agree you grunt like a caveman.

DALE. A constipated one.

WADDY. I can't believe it… *(Sits on the sofa.)* I'm really dead.

SNYDER. That you are.

WADDY. You were telling the truth about that whole curse thing?

ANGIE. Three months to the day we first kissed. I'm sorry, Waddy.

WADDY. We were married for three months. I died in mid-romp. *(Sighs. Slaps his leg.)* Well, I guess there are worse ways to go.

SNYDER. It does give new meaning to the term 'Lucky Stiff.'

WADDY. *(Crosses to the bed.)* Good one. *(He 'high-fives' Snyder.)*

ANGIE. Excuse me? Widow in the room?!

WADDY. Sorry, Angie. Move over. Give me room.

(Waddy tries to squeeze into the crowded bed with the others. Angie growls in frustration, as she disappears under the covers to climb out of the bed. She tightens the robe around her as she sits at the foot of the crowded bed.)

ANGIE. I don't think you boys appreciate how difficult this is on me! I just lost another husband! And I can't…I can't even cry about it…

SNYDER. Easy, sweetheart. You got this.

JARED. Yeah. Like familiar territory, you know?

ANGIE. That doesn't make it any easier. I'm the Angela of Death. There's even a Black Widow website in my honor!

JARED. *(Whispers to Dale.)* Better not tell her about the video game.

ANGIE. Arrrrh! I hate this curse!

SNYDER. I know, babe.

(Angie moves to the dead body and sighs. She takes a pine tree air freshener out of her pocket and hangs it on the big toes. Then grabs a can of air freshener from the mantel and starts spraying the body.)

WADDY. Really? Is that necessary?

SNYDER. More than necessary.

JARED. Mandatory, dude.

DALE. What they said.

WADDY. Well, I may be gone, but I still have to say, being married to you, Angie, was the best three months of my life.

DALE. It was the last three months of mine.

JARED. Hey, mine, too!

ANGIE. *(Broken-hearted.)* But is it worth it? Three exciting, exquisite months in exchange for the rest of your life?

DALE. *(Quickly.)* Yes.

SNYDER. Absolutely.

JARED. For sure.

WADDY. Wouldn't have it any other way.

DALE. It's not so bad. I get to see your face in a little more than forever.

ANGIE. That's sweet. But you all got the easy way out. I have to watch you die, then wait for the next guy to fall in love with.

JARED. Sounds like a soap opera, *All My Cadavers.*

(*Snyder smacks him.*)

JARED. Ow!

ANGIE. But this is one soap opera I can never turn off. I…I better go call someone.

(*She exits. Snyder calls after her.*)

SNYDER. Press star three. You have the coroner on speed dial.

(*Snyder watches her exit with sadness. Waddy, Dale and Jared jostle in the bed.*)

WADDY. Scooch over a bit.

JARED. Stop hogging the sheets, bro!

DALE. What is that? Get it off me!

BLACKOUT

END OF ACT ONE, SCENE 4

ACT ONE
Scene 5

(The four dead husbands freeze in the bed, as Narrator enters, UL.)

NARRATOR. Curses affect the soul in the same way as lies, violence and prejudices, which are curses in their own right. They each develop their own momentum. Starting off slowly, even softly, then gradually, silently skewing our focus and dominating our attention. Before we know it, every waking hour is built around the fear they grow from and feed upon. Until everything speeds up, like the last fifteen minutes of the movie 'Goodfellas'.

(Throughout the following, they gradually exit, one at a time. Leaving only Dale in the bed.)

NARRATOR. And so it was with Angie. She had three full years to mourn Jared before the curse pulled her lips in a new direction. Then the time between last goodbye, and next first kiss grew shorter and shorter. Two years. Then one. Then six months. Then three. It was the most vicious of cycles, and one that was taking its toll on Angie. Her biggest fear was that she would kiss an EMT as he came to pick up the body of her most recent ex-husband. Yet, the presence of her old lovers made the curse almost bearable.

(NARRATOR exits, UR. Angie enters UL and smiles at Dale in the bed.)

ANGIE. Hey, do you mind?

(Dale stretches and climbs out as Angie begins making the bed.)

DALE. This is nice. Almost like old times.

ANGIE. If you mean, me making the bed and cleaning up, while you stand there watching? Yeah. Good times.

DALE. It wasn't all bad, was it? You and me?

ANGIE. *(Softens.)* It wasn't bad at all, Dale. It was wonderful. You were so kind, and sweet, and funny.

DALE. And a better lover than the others….

ANGIE. *(Ignoring him.)* I think I need new pillows….

DALE. I said I was a better…

ANGIE. I heard what you said. And you heard how loudly I ignored you.

DALE. *(Like a hurt little boy.)* So I wasn't your best?

ANGIE. Dale, I loved you. You were everything I ever wanted in a husband.

DALE. Until the next one came along.

ANGIE. It doesn't mean that I love you any less. Or love them more. And even when I'm giddy with love over my next husband, the pain I feel over losing you, over losing each one of you, doesn't fade in the least. One happiness and more than a dozen catastrophic heartbreaks. If that isn't a curse, I don't know what is.

DALE. I'm sorry, Angie. Sorry you have to go through all this.

ANGIE. That's the curse talking. If it wasn't for that evil spell, you probably wouldn't have given me a second look.

DALE. That's not true. All the curse did was rush the process. I would have loved you with or without the curse.

ANGIE. I wish I could kiss you now.

DALE. So do I. Can I ask you one more question? Did I at least make the top ten?

ANGIE. Dale!

DALE. Hey, I'm a corpse with a crush. Give me something here.

ANGIE. *(Whispers.)* Yes. You were definitely in my top ten.

OTHER EXES. *(Their heads pop in Upstage.)* We heard that!

ANGIE. See the kind of trouble you get me in?

DALE. But I'm worth it. *(Pumps his fist in the air.)* Top ten!

> *(A KNOCK on the door, DR.)*

DALE. Who is that?

ANGIE. How should I know? It's a door. Not a window.

DALE. You should probably answer it.

ANGIE. *(Annoyed.)* You think?

> *(She smacks the pillow into place, then crosses to the DR door, as Dale heads off UL.)*

DALE. Top ten!!!

> *(Angie shakes her head and opens the door to...)*

NARRATOR/LAGRANGE. You see, I'm not simply a disinterested party in this story. I'm also...

ANGIE. Mr. LaGrange. I was expecting you.

NARRATOR/LAGRANGE. I am sure you were, Mrs. Luffnell-Sheffield-Simon-Rodriguez-Umbartu-Smith-Kracowski-Fitzgerald-Cochello-Duff-Thrombottom-Usaki-Crestwood-Watterson.

ANGIE. Come in. Make yourself at home.

NARRATOR/LAGRANGE. With the number of calls my company makes to this address, it does feel like my second home. *(Notices the newer portrait on the mantel.)* Who is that?

ANGIE. Waddy. Mr. Peytona.

NARRATOR/LAGRANGE. And he would be?

ANGIE. My new husband.

NARRATOR/LAGRANGE. Congratulations. And Mr. Peytona is...?

ANGIE. Recently deceased.

NARRATOR/LAGRANGE. Of course, he is.

ANGIE. That's a rather unsympathetic statement.

NARRATOR/LAGRANGE. Forgive me. Was Mr. Peytona ill?

ANGIE. Not at all. He was the picture of health. Unnervingly so.

NARRATOR/LAGRANGE. Excuse me for asking, but if your husband was so healthy, why do you have the bed in the living room?

ANGIE. He was also rather affectionate.

NARRATOR/LAGRANGE. And by affectionate, you mean...?

ANGIE. Six times a day for the past three months.

NARRATOR/LAGRANGE. That must have been...

ANGIE. Exhausting, yes. Now that he's dead, I can at least catch my breath... *(Catches herself.)* I suppose you're shocked.

NARRATOR/LAGRANGE. More in awe than shock. Six times a day. What was his secret, if I may ask?

ANGIE. Fertilizer.

NARRATOR/LAGRANGE. I beg your pardon. For a second there, I thought you said...

ANGIE. Fertilizer. As in that wonderful smell even a boatload of Febreze and industrial air deodorizers can't get rid of. It was polite of you not to notice.

NARRATOR/LAGRANGE. Politeness is part of my job.

ANGIE. He even bought me this necklace for our one month anniversary.

(She pulls a chain from around her neck, with a tree-shaped piece of green cardboard dangling from it.)

NARRATOR/LAGRANGE. That's an air freshener. I have one of those hanging from my car mirror.

ANGIE. Waddy was sweet, but less than fragrant. *(Shakes off the memory.)* Anyway, I believe you have something for me?

THE KISS ME CURSE

NARRATOR/LAGRANGE. Well, as frustrated as my company is, we can find no cause for denying payment for your late husband's recent passing. Forgive me, I mean your earlier late husband. Mr. Watterson. Not your latest late husband. *(Pulls out a check.)* Here is a check for ten million dollars, the full amount of the life insurance policy you rather conveniently took out the day you were married.

ANGIE. Just put it on the mantel with the others.

NARRATOR/LAGRANGE. This is a ten million dollar check!

ANGIE. They all are. I should probably put them in the bank soon. It is so hard to find time between planning weddings, then funerals, weddings and funerals, weddings and funerals.

NARRATOR/LAGRANGE. Not to mention the six times a day living room acrobatics.

ANGIE. May he rest in peace… now that I finally have a chance to. Is there anything else?

NARRATOR/LAGRANGE. All we ask is that you choose not to do business with the Steadfast Life Insurance Company in the future. Paying out three death benefits in two years is murder on our bottom line. No pun intended.

ANGIE. Don't worry. I believe in spreading the grief. No more than three multi-million dollar life insurance policies with any one company.

NARRATOR/LAGRANGE. You must be exceedingly rich.

ANGIE. You think I married fourteen husbands for the money?

NARRATOR/LAGRANGE. The thought did cross my mind. As well as the underwriters. And half the detectives on the local Police Force.

ANGIE. I marry for love. Every time. Is that so hard to believe?

NARRATOR/LAGRANGE. Not for me. But then again, I also believe in honest politicians, and that someday they will finish construction work on the freeway downtown.

ANGIE. Have you ever been in love, Mr. LaGrange?

NARRATOR/LAGRANGE. I sell insurance. On the Ideal Husband Index, that makes me a step below dentists and cesspool cleaners.

ANGIE. Well, I have been in love. Totally, magically, obsessively in love. I have been seduced and smitten. Enthralled, entranced and enraptured by fourteen of the most wonderful men God ever put on this earth. Every time my heart soars and sings, it shatters again. Tasting love, then finding myself empty and broken three months later. Love, wince and repeat. No amount of money is worth that.

NARRATOR/LAGRANGE. Ten million dollars.

ANGIE. You can keep it.

NARRATOR/LAGRANGE. Can I?

ANGIE. I was being rhetorical. Put the check on the mantel.

NARRATOR/LAGRANGE. I do have one more question. Why are you always on the other side of the room when you speak to me?

ANGIE. I don't want you to kiss me.

NARRATOR/LAGRANGE. Proof again the Ideal Husband Index is cruel to insurance salesmen.

ANGIE. It's not that. I just don't want to get a check from *your* life insurance policy one day.

NARRATOR/LAGRANGE. Thank you. I think.

(He nods, turns to the door, UR)

NARRATOR/LAGRANGE. Mrs. Luffnell-Sheffield-Simon-Rodriguez-Umbartu-Smith-Kracowski-Fitzgerald-Cochello-Duff-Thrombottom-Usaki-Crestwood-Watterson?

ANGIE. You forgot Peytona.

NARRATOR/LAGRANGE. Mrs. Luffnell-Sheffield-Simon-Rodriguez-Umbartu-Smith-Kracowski…

ANGIE. Call me Angie.

NARRATOR/LAGRANGE. Angie…Can I ask you something personal? Just between us?

The Kiss Me Curse

ANGIE. There is no us. Because if you start thinking there is an us, three months later you won't be a you anymore and then the us will be just me, while you'll be just another box in Baggage Hold.

NARRATOR/LAGRANGE. Incomprehensibility aside…Are your kisses really that irresistible?

ANGIE. Yes. It's a curse.

NARRATOR/LAGRANGE. I…I imagine it would be…

(As Narrator and Angie are pulled toward each other. Dale enters and jumps in between them.)

DALE. Not again! Guys, give me a hand here!

JARED. *(Entering DL.)* Been there. Done that. Got a T-shirt.

SNYDER. *(Entering UR.)* It doesn't help. The curse is too strong.

(All the husbands stand between them, waving their arms. Of course, Narrator/Lagrange doesn't see them, as Angie is being pulled forward with the strength of the curse.)

DALE. Angie. Think about what you're doing!

(Angie is mesmerized. Moves step-by-step toward an equally smitten LaGrange.)

WADDY. *(Entering DR.)* Maybe I can help.

(He jumps in between them and lifts his arms. All the others immediately grab their noses. The spell overpowered by the smell.)

NARRATOR/LAGRANGE. What is that odor?

ANGIE. Ugh…a wake-up call. You should go.

NARRATOR/LAGRANGE. Angie, I…

ANGIE. Your lips are quivering, and that usually means I'll be putting your portrait above the mantel and your body in my cemetery condo three months from now. Is that what you want?

NARRATOR/LAGRANGE. You have a cemetery condo?

ANGIE. I have three vacancies left. You don't want to be one of them.

NARRATOR/LAGRANGE. I suppose I better go. *(Grabs the door handle.)* Six times a day for three months? I really must invest in some fertilizer…

(NARRATOR/LAGRANGE exits UL.)

JARED. Phew. That was close.

SNYDER. *(Nodding to Waddy.)* Phew is right.

DALE. What were you thinking, sweetheart? You know you shouldn't get within lip distance of men.

ANGIE. I wasn't thinking! I'm cursed, remember?! I'm a stupid, empty, selfish, mouth-to-mouth murderer! And that's all I'll ever be! And I don't need a posse of dead exes to remind me of that!

(She storms off, DR.)

WADDY. *(Sarcastically. To Dale.)* Good one.

BLACKOUT

END OF ACT ONE, SCENE 5

ACT ONE
Scene 6

AT RISE: The living room scene once more. The bed is gone. Waddy's face has been removed from the portrait above the mantel, leaving a blank cut-out where the last husband's face was. Narrator enters. Tries to shed his Mr. LaGrange persona.

NARRATOR. It's okay. I'm fine now. I'm not even thinking about Angie's eyes… *(Dreamily.)* Her soft…lush…enticing lips… *(Catches himself. Straightens.)* Anyway, I wasn't the only surprise our winsome widow would get that week. Two more would soon follow. One more dangerous than the last.

   (KNOCK on the door, DL.)

NARRATOR. There's the first one now. Right on time.

   (Narrator exits DR as Waddy runs on UL.)

WADDY. Someone's at the door!

   (Angie enters right behind him. Tying the sash on her silk robe.)

ANGIE. *(Yawning)* I heard.

WADDY. You should get that.

ANGIE. Probably. Considering I'm the only one here with actual hands. *(Shakes off her sleepiness.)* Why do men always feel the need to say the most obvious things?

WADDY. Helping?

ANGIE. Hardly.

   (She throws open the door, DL.)

WADDY. Aaaaaaaaaarrgh!

(Waddy screeches and runs off UR. Angie watches him flee in confusion.)

SLIGO. Hey, I'm standin' here?!

ANGIE. Sorry. Can I help you?

(SLIGO NEWCASTLE pushes his way in, looking every bit the two-bit thug in a cheap suit, from an even cheaper B movie. He shoves past Angie and begins casing the joint.)

SLIGO. Naw. I'm here to help you'se. Nice digs.

ANGIE. Do I know you, Mr...?

SLIGO. Newcastle. Sligo Newcastle. Maybe ya seen my name around?

ANGIE. Sorry.

SLIGO. Don't get out much, do ya? I'm da guy what runs the lower east side of Pewee Valley.

ANGIE. Oh. Are you a politician?

SLIGO. Politician. Ha! That's rich. Me, I'm the kinda guy who's honest about his dishonesty. You could say I'm in the missing persons racket.

ANGIE. You find them?

SLIGO. Naw. I'm usually on the other side of that transaction.

ANGIE. You're a criminal.

SLIGO. Yeah, but that don't look as good on my business cards. *(Looking around.)* I'm surprised old Waddy didn't mention me.

ANGIE. I kept him pretty busy. If you don't mind my asking, what kind of name is Sligo?

SLIGO. Dutch.

ANGIE. No, it's not.

SLIGO. Micronesian then.

ANGIE. Micronesian?

SLIGO. Hey, my mother loved men of all nationalities. Sometimes in rapid succession. *(Mumbling.)* Sure made Father's Day confusing. But enough about me, dollface. Let's talk about your hubby.

ANGIE. Which one?

SLIGO. Waddy. I been lookin' for him.

ANGIE. *(Looking around.)* You just missed him.

SLIGO. Yeah? I heard he was dead?

ANGIE. That's um…what I meant.

SLIGO. Funny. 'Cuz my nostrils detect a familiar Peytona aroma. Fertilizer was his biz. As well as his perfume. Yet you go and tell me old Waddy is no more. So who am I supposed to believe? You, or my nostrils?

ANGIE. You knew the Fertilizer King. The one thing you can say about him was that he lingered.

SLIGO. This is true. So he's dead, eh? Who went and whacked old Waddy?

ANGIE. He did it himself. More cracked than whacked. A…um, gymnastics accident.

SLIGO. See now, that there is a shame. 'Cuz old Waddy owed me a whole wad of cash. So in the interests of free enterprise, I'm here to collect what's mine, by any means necessary. You his old lady?

ANGIE. If you mean, am I his wife? Or more precisely, his widow? Then yes. I am.

SLIGO. Well, then you'se and me got us some business to undertake here. *(Gestures towards her silk robe.)* I like your accouterments, by the way.

ANGIE. Thank you. If I knew you were stopping by, I would have gotten even more…um, 'accoutered.'

SLIGO. You'se sure talk swell.

ANGIE. That makes one of us.

(She moves away from him. But he pursues her, standing uncomfortably close.)

SLIGO. A gal with a smart mouth. I like that. Up until the time I don't. Then you'se better watch out. But seein' as how you'se is his closest living and breakable relation, I'm thinkin' you'se is on the hook for old Waddy's bite. Get me?

ANGIE. Not even remotely.

SLIGO. Let me put it in a language you'se can understand. I'm here as a concerned citizen what don't want to see nothin' bad happen to a classy dame like yourself.

ANGIE. Thank you for your concern, but I can take care of myself.

SLIGO. Or alternately, you can be taken care of, if you'se know what I mean. Like maybe you'se could take a spill off some stolen pontoon boat in the Ohio River. Like around midnight some day soon.

ANGIE. I can swim.

SLIGO. Not with hundred pound cement shoes on.

ANGIE. And the odds of that would be?

SLIGO. Pretty darn good. Dependin' on how long it takes you'se to come up with my dough.

ANGIE. Are you threatening me, Mr. Newcastle?

SLIGO. Threatenin' is such an aggressive word. Let's just say I am informing you'se of the tragic consequences likely to befall any and all who unwisely refuse to let me get my way in all things.

ANGIE. You're right. That's much less aggressive.

SLIGO. Listen, dollface. I'm not such a bad guy. I would never hurt a woman. Unless there was money in it. Or she did something to tick me off. *(Beat.)* Or she made that strange sucking sound with her teeth. You know what I mean? *'thweck. thwack thwack.'* I hate anyone what does that. It's an idiosyncrasy of mine.

ANGIE. We all have our faults.

SLIGO. Hey, I didn't say it was a fault. I said it was an idiosyncrasy. You'se should learn to listen better!

ANGIE. Sorry.

SLIGO. Apology accepted, dollface. Now then, while you'se is waiting to make the correct decision that I know you'se will do, I gotta remove myself and stare at something porcelain for a few.

ANGIE. Excuse me?

SLIGO. You'se have a Little Thug's Room in this place?

ANGIE. Oh, porcelain. Got it. Down the hall. First door on your left. And please try not to steal the soap while you're in there.

SLIGO. Funny dame. I can see what Waddy saw in you'se. That, and those decent-sized bazoombas you got under your robe there.

ANGIE. How almost charming of you to say.

SLIGO. Hey, that's what people love about me.

(Exits, UL. Once he's gone, Angie turns and yells...)

ANGIE. Waddy Peytona!

(Waddy pops his head in sheepishly.)

WADDY. Uh, yes, dear?

ANGIE. Don't 'Yes, dear' me. Would you mind explaining why I have a Sopranos wannabe in my bathroom?

WADDY. Well, um, as he said...I sort of, you know, in some sense perhaps...owe him a little bit of well, money, kind of, like.

ANGIE. How much is 'a little bit?'

WADDY. A hundred and ninety.

ANGIE. That's all?

WADDY. ...thousand...

ANGIE. A hundred and ninety thousand dollars?!

WADDY. Plus the vig.

ANGIE. The fig?

WADDY. The vig that Sligo charges. Twenty percent a week. Unfortunately, I got a bit behind on the payments since I was so distracted with our honeymoon and such.

ANGIE. Distracted?

WADDY. Six times a day for the past three months. You have to admit that was pretty distracting.

ANGIE. You borrowed money from a loanshark and didn't tell me? I could kill you!

WADDY. Well, technically, you already did.

(Snyder & Jared enter, DR & DL.)

SNYDER. What's all the hollering about?

ANGIE. My dear departed husband here gangstered up, and now I have a Sligo Newcastle in my Little Thug's Room. *(Pause.)* Wow. I never thought I would ever say a sentence like that…

(Dale runs on, UR.)

DALE. Sligo Newcastle?! The Pewee Valley mob boss? Did he threaten you?

ANGIE. Not at all. *(In Sligo's voice.)* He merely informed me of the tragic consequences likely to befall any and all who don't let him get his way in all things. *(Pause.)* Plus a mention of the Ohio River and cement shoes. Or Jimmy Choos. He's kind of hard to understand…

DALE. He's going to hurt our Angie!

WADDY. Not if we pay him off.

SNYDER. How much are you into him for, Mister Sweet Smell of Success?

WADDY. A hundred and ninety large.

ANGIE. Plus the fig.

DALE. You borrowed a fig?

WADDY. Not a fig. The vig.

DALE. Well, that clarifies things not much.

JARED. The vig, dude. The vigorish. The cut. The take. The juice.

DALE. *(Sighs.)* I have never felt as middle-class white suburban male as I do now…

WADDY. The vig is the interest a loanshark charges. And it's uh… built up a little while Angie and I were…you know…

JARED. We know. We saw. We shuddered.

SNYDER. So how big is your vig, you pig?

WADDY. Well, three months at twenty percent a week… About two-point-eight.

DALE. Two-point-eight what?

WADDY. Million.

ANGIE. I'll kill him!

WADDY. It's not that bad! Between the insurance money and the assets from my business…

ANGIE. What assets? According to your books, you are cash poor.

WADDY. There's the warehouse full of manure.

DALE. Manure is not a liquid asset.

WADDY. Would you want it to be?

SNYDER. Look, I say we just pay Sligo off and be done with it. The guy's bad news. Best to get him out of our hair, and as far away from our Angie as possible.

JARED. Yeah. You don't want to mess with a guy like that.

DALE. Or…

ANGIE. Or what, Dale?

DALE. Or maybe we could do something about it. Maybe we are looking at this curse all wrong. What if you were to use your powers for good, instead of evil?

ANGIE. They're not powers.

DALE. Of course they are. Think of all the bad guys you could take out with one little smooch.

JARED. I get it, dude. With great lips comes great responsibility.

SNYDER. Did you leave your brain in purgatory or something?

DALE. There's a purgatory?

SNYDER. I was being ironic.

ANGIE. What are you saying, Dale?

DALE. This Sligo Newcastle is a bad man. He hurts people. Probably kills them too.

WADDY. Only a few dozen. He has his victim's names tattooed on his left shoulder. *(Shudders.)* And a little way down his back…

DALE. So why not be Avenging Angie, and help clean up the world a bit?

ANGIE. By…

DALE. Kissing him.

SNYDER. Are you brain dead?! You want my wife to kiss that mobster?!

WADDY. She's my wife too, and I say 'nuh-uh. No way!'

ANGIE. *(Pause.)* Maybe Dale's right.

SNYDER. Am I hearing what I'm hearing? 'Cuz it sure sounded like you said, 'maybe Dale's right.'

ANGIE. Think about it. All I have ever done is cause pain. Maybe it is time I made something positive out of this curse.

JARED. Righteous! Like you could be a cursed crusader. The Lipinator. Taking a smooch out of crime!

DALE. This guy has made more ghosts than you, and not by playing bumper face!

SNYDER. Bumper face?

DALE. Lip hockey. Tongue tag.

JARED. Have I been dead that long? We used to just call it necking.

SNYDER. Angie, babe, I think you should seriously think about what you're thinking about here.

ANGIE. I already have.

(Sligo reenters from UL, wipes his hands on Angie's sofa.)

SLIGO. You already have, what?

SNYDER. Tell me that's not the guy my old lady's gotta kiss? I'm not liking this at all.

ANGIE. I already have decided to pay you your money, Mr. Newcastle.

SLIGO. Call me Sligo, dollface. 'Specially now that you'se is being so reasonable-like. Course you'se ain't heard my final number yet.

ANGIE. One hundred and ninety large. Plus the fig.

ALL OTHERS. The VIG!

ANGIE. Sorry. The vig.

SLIGO. The vig's pretty big. Took me some weeks to track old Waddy back to you. So I'm thinkin' that vig's up to a good three million by now.

WADDY. Three million! He's lying!

SNYDER. Gee, a criminal who doesn't tell the truth. What are the odds of that?

WADDY. Do the right thing, Angie. Kiss him!

ANGIE. I...I...

SLIGO. What? Do I intimidate you'se? Do I make you'se stutter? *(Smiles.)* It's understandable. A hot dame like yourself. All alone in this big, fancy house. You'se could use a man around here to watch over you'se.

ANGIE. Thanks. But it's crowded enough around here as it is. Why don't you just take a check from the mantel.

(He crosses upstage to the mantel. Picks up the check the insurance agent left.).

SLIGO. This here is ten million dollars.

ANGIE. They all are.

SLIGO. You think I'm some kind of idiot? Nobody keeps checks for ten mil lying around.

ANGIE. Those are insurance payments. The actual estates are worth even more than that.

SLIGO. Yeah? *(Looking at the other checks.)* So all these checks. Millions of dollars... What say you'se just sign them all over to me, and you'se and me call it square, eh?

ANGIE. You want me to sign over sixty million dollars to you for a three million dollar debt?

SLIGO. Call it a tip. Or a good investment in your future.

ANGIE. My future?

SLIGO. Ensuring you have one.

ANGIE. How do I know you won't whack me the moment I sign over all those checks to you?

SLIGO. Now why would I go and do I bad thing like that?

ANGIE. I don't know. Maybe because you're robbing me. Because I've seen your face. To stop me from testifying against you.

SLIGO. Do I look like the kinda guy who'd whack an unarmed dame just for her money, and maybe my own peace of mind? *(Pause. No reply.)* I said, do I look like the kinda guy who'd whack an unarmed dame just for her money and my own peace of mind? *(Pause. No reply.)* I'm lookin' for an answer here!

ANGIE. *(Backing away.)* I...I guess not.

(His face darkens. He crosses over to her, menacingly.)

SLIGO. Then you'se ain't a real good judge of character.

(He pulls a gun from his pocket.)

SLIGO. Now what say you'se sign these here checks so's we can quickly terminate dis somewhat uncomfortable business relationship, eh?

SNYDER. Angie!!

(All her dead husbands leap forward to rush to her defense, swinging at Sligo, who does not see them. All their punches miss, as if their ghostly fists pass right through him.)

SLIGO. Is there a breeze in here or somethin'?

ANGIE. Will you grant me one last request?

SLIGO. *(Shrugs.)* Sure thing, dollface.

ANGIE. Kiss me.

SLIGO. You'se want me to kiss you'se? Now?

ANGIE. I don't think I've ever felt the need to kiss anyone more.

SLIGO. Must be my innate animal magnetism. What the hell. Pucker up, princess.

ANGIE. *(Grabs his lapels.)* I warn you. I can be quite addictive.

SLIGO. Bring it on, sugar lips.

(He hovers menacingly over her.)

SUDDEN BLACKOUT

(From the darkness, a GUNSHOT, and a SCREAM.)

DALE. *ANGIE!!!!*

CURTAIN

END OF ACT ONE

ACT TWO
Scene 1

NARRATOR. When we're young, we look at the vast expanse of time before us, and it seems endless. We wait forever for Christmas to come each year. Even longer to get our license or set out on the long road of adulthood. Yet once on the other side of that curve, with more years behind us than ahead, we realize how little time we actually have on this Earth. We wake one morning in dull surprise, realizing we have more memories accumulated than dreams left to realize, as the fiercely seductive embrace of oblivion has crept ever closer. *(Smiles.)* But that doesn't mean the fun is over…

AT RISE: The living room as before. Angie's body sprawled awkwardly on the sofa. Dale, Snyder and Jared rush in.

DALE.   Angie! Angie, wake up!

JARED.   She's not moving.

SNYDER.   Give her some air! Angie, babe. Wake up.

   (Angie's eyes slowly flutter open.)

ANGIE.   *(Yawning.)* Can't you guys give me even one moment's peace?

SNYDER.   Sorry, but no.

DALE.   He's at it again!

ANGIE.   Who?

SNYDER.   Who d'ya think?

   (Sligo enters, shoving Waddy in front of him.)

SLIGO.   Move it, stink boy.

The Kiss Me Curse

(Only then do we notice the urn on the mantel and Sligo's face now with Angie in the portrait.)

ANGIE. Sligo! Play nice.

SLIGO. Nice ain't in my character. 'Specially with these petrified poltergeists hangin' around.

DALE. We are not poltergeists. We are disembodied spirits!

SLIGO. Hey, 'scuse me for bein' eloquent. Now what say you'se shut your pie holes and go out and haunt somethin', eh?

DALE. See what we have to *not* live with?!

ANGIE. Don't blame me. Whose big idea was it for me to kiss him in the first place?

(One by one, they all turn to Dale.)

DALE. Uh, it seemed like a good idea at the time. I mean, with great lips come great responsibility and all that. Right? *(The others only glare at him.)* I guess I didn't think it through...

SNYDER. I guess you didn't.

ANGIE. How come none of you realized that my doing in the bad guy meant you'd be stuck with him for all eternity?

JARED. Uh, maybe we weren't that bright?

SNYDER. Now we have to spend the afterlife with The Ghostfather here.

SLIGO. The Ghostfather. I kinda like that. Whatta ya say, fertilizer boy?

WADDY. Angie?

ANGIE. Hey, you guys wanted me to kiss him, knowing I'd fall hopelessly in love with the big brute.

SLIGO. Love you too, dollface.

ANGIE. Thanks, pumpkin.

SLIGO. Hey, I told you'se! I don't like you callin' me pumpkin in fronta the boys.

ANGIE. The curse means I have to love you. It doesn't mean I have to listen to anything you say. *(With a mischievous smirk.)* …pumpkin.

ALL OTHERS. *(Like teasing children.)* She called you pumpkin! She called you pumpkin!

SLIGO. I'm warnin' you'se guys!

ANGIE. Take it easy… *(Giggling.)* …pumpkin.

ALL OTHERS. *(Like teasing children.)* She called you pumpkin! She called you pumpkin!

SLIGO. I'm gonna kill you'se all!

SNYDER. Already missed that bus, pumpkin. We've got no money to steal. Or bodies to break.

JARED. Seriously, dude. Threats don't mean diddly to the deceased.

WADDY. Yeah. You can't intimidate us.

SLIGO. Grrrrrrrrr…

WADDY. Okay. Maybe just a little. Like when you make that mean growly face and all.

SNYDER. Stand up for yourself, Waddy. He's nothing but a disembodied bully now.

DALE. Nothing but vapor.

SLIGO. Oh, yeah?!

(Sligo swats his arms around angrily, affecting nothing. The others step back and mock as he vents his frustration.)

JARED. Chill, dude. You're like, gonna bust an aura or something.

SNYDER. See, Waddy? He's harmless.

SLIGO. I'll show you harmless! Grrrraaaa-AAARRRGHH!!!

(Bursting with rage, he stretches out his arms, strains and eventually picks up a throw pillow from the sofa and tosses it across the room. The others are stunned.)

DALE. Did you see that?!

ANGIE. I don't believe it…

JARED. We're all like, spirits and stuff. We can't like, touch or move anything!

SLIGO. *(Pleased with himself.)* Tell that to the pillow.

WADDY. How…how'd you do that?

SLIGO. You ain't never seen The Ghostfather before. Now, we're gonna make some changes 'round here in the afterlife. You'se guys are gonna show a little respect.

SNYDER. Or what? We gonna have a pillow fight?

SLIGO. You want a piece of me?

SNYDER. There ain't no pieces of you anymore. They're in that urn over there. Angie had you cremated so your business associates wouldn't peepee on your grave.

JARED. Leadership issues, man. So hard to get good help these days.

SNYDER. All that bluster, and you just made an ash of yourself.

SLIGO. I've had about enough of you!

ANGIE. *(Jumping in between them.)* Boys, please! I love you all, but you don't know how hard it is to listen to all my dead husbands whine and moan and argue twenty-four hours a day. It's exhausting!

SLIGO. Sorry, dollface. Don't mean to get you all riled up or nothin'. Just tell 'corpse boy' here to get outta my face!

SNYDER. You ain't got a face. That's in that urn over there too.

(DOORBELL Rings.)

DALE. There's someone at the door.

WADDY. You should probably answer it.

ANGIE. *(Angie crosses DL to answer it.)* Aaaaaah!

WADDY. Well, she should…

JARED. Doors are harsh, man.

(Angie throws open the door. Stands there stunned.)

OFFSTAGE VOICE. What's wrong, Angie? You look like you've seen a ghost.

(Angie steps back, clearly shaken.)

JARED. I can't believe it…

ANGIE. It…it can't be…

DALE. What can't be?

(In walks Maggie, looking older but still as bitter. She cocks her head, as if she hears something.)

JARED. That's Maggie.

SNYDER. Saggy Maggie?!

MAGGIE. Come on, fellas. Nobody calls me Saggy Maggie anymore.

WADDY. Wait, she can see us?!

MAGGIE. No, but I can hear you. Sounds like you have quite a collection, Angie. Glad to see you've kept yourself busy since high school.

SLIGO. Wait… You mean this is da broad what cursed my little Angie?! And made us all like this?! Why I oughta whack her!

(Maggie picks up Sligo's urn from the mantel. She shakes it, and Sligo's body shakes wildly every time she does.)

MAGGIE. Oooh! That one sounds like a real tough guy. You obviously married him for his intellect.

(She shakes the urn again, causing Sligo to gyrate uncontrollably.)

SLIGO. Why, I oughta…! Give me a pillow!

(Maggie puts down the urn and grabs a pillow from the sofa, playing 'keep away' with Sligo.)

MAGGIE. Somebody want this?

SLIGO. Gimme that, you witch!

MAGGIE. Oooh. You've got a feisty one there. Come get the pillow. That's a good ghostie. Come get the pillow.

SLIGO. I hate this dame!

JARED. Same old Maggie.

MAGGIE. *(Cocking her head to listen. Her voice softens.)* That sounds like my Jared. How have you been, honey? *(Sadly.)* How was Prom?

JARED. Like, ouch, Maggie.

MAGGIE. I…I'm sorry, Jared.

ANGIE. What are you doing here, Maggie?

MAGGIE. What else do high school friends do after they haven't seen each other for a long time? I'm gloating. *(Sits.)* Aren't you going to offer me a drink, Angie?

DALE. I'll get the arsenic.

MAGGIE. Easy, fellas. It's not good to hold grudges. That's what my therapist always tells me.

ANGIE. Your therapist?

MAGGIE. He specializes in anger management issues. Do you have anything you're angry about, sunshine?

ANGIE. You're kidding, right? Your little curse has cost me more than a dozen dead husbands.

ALL HUSBANDS. *(Various Comments.)* Yeah… You did this to us… Witch…

MAGGIE. I'm sensing an air of hostility in this room. *(Sniffs.)* And fertilizer… *(Happily.)* So other than the sixteen weddings and funerals…what have you been doing with yourself, girlfriend?

ANGIE. You know what I've been doing with myself. Falling apart over all these beautiful, crazy, frustrating men you've made me fall in love with. And then watch die.

MAGGIE. That was rather bitchy of me, don't you think? But look at you. Shy, lonely little Angie. Kills more people than mad cow disease. I guess that is what happens when you steal the wrong person's Prom date.

ANGIE. You ruined my life!

MAGGIE. And you ruined mine! Jared and I had a good thing going! At least until those lips of yours came along.

ANGIE. So you had him killed?

MAGGIE. It was Prom!

JARED. She's got a point there.

OTHER EXES. Shut up!

ANGIE. Do you know how many lives you've shattered? Thanks to you, I'm more deadly to my mates than a praying mantis!

MAGGIE. Then you should have kept your kisses to yourself! *(Composing herself.)* Anyway, that's why I'm here. My therapist says it's important to let go of old grudges. Forgive and forget. Resentment causes wrinkles.

ANGIE. So you are going to remove the curse?

MAGGIE. I wish I could. I really do. It would be so cleansing for me. Did I mention that resentment causes wrinkles?

ANGIE. The curse, Maggie...

MAGGIE. Oh, right. I'd really like to help you out with all that, but I can't.

ANGIE. You can't? Or won't?

MAGGIE. Can't, it seems. Not all curses have an escape hatch. There's no do-over with this one.

ANGIE. So...all this will never end?

MAGGIE. Sorry. My bad.

ANGIE. I'll keep kissing and killing and kissing and killing until I'm ninety?

MAGGIE. Maybe even then. You know how frisky those Assisted Living places can be.

ANGIE. *(Collapsing.)* I'm doomed.

ALL EXES. We're all doomed.

MAGGIE. I'm afraid so. *(Brightens.)* But my therapist was right. I do feel so much better now that we have had our little talk and cleared the air!

ANGIE. That's it? You're just going to walk out and leave me like this?

MAGGIE. Sure looks that way.

ANGIE. But that's evil!

MAGGIE. Kinda. But again, I was new at the whole curse thing back then. *(Crosses to the door.)* And now that we've put the past behind us, neither of us have to worry about those pesky old wrinkles anymore, do we? Have a nice life!

DALE. *(Thinking quickly.)* Wait, Angie. You're not going to let her go with that thing on her face, are you?

MAGGIE. What did he say? What thing on my face?

SNYDER. *(Picking up on it.)* Yeah. It'd be pretty embarrassing to walk outside like that.

DALE. Almost cruel.

SNYDER. But it would serve her right.

MAGGIE. *(Wiping at her face.)* What? What's on my face?

JARED. That gross crusty thing on your upper lip. It's like, seriously gnarly.

MAGGIE. *(Wiping even more frantically.)* Ugh. Did I get it? Is it still there?

WADDY. Yup. Right by your mouth.

DALE. Disgusting. You should really help her, Angie.

MAGGIE. Yes, Angie. Get it off me!

ANGIE. But I don't see anything?

SNYDER. Look closer. It's right on her upper lip.

(Angie leans closer to inspect Maggie's face.)

MAGGIE. Get it off me!

DALE. Sligo, would you do the honors?

SLIGO. With pleasure.

(With a hefty growl, Sligo pushes the two women's head together, forcing their lips to touch. STAGE LIGHTS FLICKER, as they freeze.)

SNYDER. And curse-wise, I do believe that qualifies as a kiss.

MAGGIE. Oh no….

BLACKOUT

END OF ACT TWO, SCENE 1

ACT TWO
Scene 2

NARRATOR. We cannot always choose whom we love. Sometimes the heart sends us running in directions we never expected to go. The perfect match on paper barely raises a smile, while the utterly unexpected choice: older, younger, cruder, less attractive, or wildly incompatible, quickens the pulse and sends our imagination soaring.

AT RISE: Angie's living room – One month later. The portrait over the mantel has the same husband's body beside Angie, only now with a cut out of Maggie's face pasted over it.)

NARRATOR. Yet if there is one curse we all share, it is that all love ends. Every vow of forever is destined to be broken. Every hug holds the promise of heartache. Everyone we care for will one day slip away, even as mortality forces us to slip away from them.

(Maggie lies curled up on the sofa, her back to the audience. Jared, Dale and Snyder huddle together DC, whispering.)

SNYDER. *(Softly.)* I say it's none of our business!

JARED. Snyder's right.

DALE. Of course, it's our business. Everything that concerns my wife is my business!

JARED. Dale's right.

SNYDER. First of all, she's not just your wife. She's my wife too. And Jared's.

JARED. Snyder's right.

SNYDER. Secondly, you know what this will do to Angie when she finds out? You really want to bring her more pain?

DALE. It's going to hurt however she finds out. Me, I'd rather get bad news all at once. Like tearing off a Band-Aid off, instead of tugging at it slowly.

JARED. Dale's right. Band-Aids are the worst.

SNYDER. *(To Jared.)* Will you shut up?

JARED. Uh…Right.

DALE. We have to tell her.

(Angie enters happily, UL.)

ANGIE. Tell me what?

(The three whispering ghosts try their best to look innocent, as they glance at the sleeping Maggie on the sofa.)

DALE. Uh, nothing. Nothing at all.

SNYDER. Not a thing.

ANGIE. Let me guess. Maggie was tormenting you guys with the Ouija board again. I've asked her not to do that.

DALE. Yeah. That must have been it.

SNYDER. We gotta fly.

JARED. We can fly?!

SNYDER. Move it, moron!

JARED. Oh…right.

(They scamper off, UR.)

ANGIE. No matter how many husbands I have, I'll never understand men. *(Crosses to the sofa.)* Wake up, Maggie. They have a *Bewitched* marathon on Channel thirty-four. *(Jostles her.)* Maggie?

(As she tugs at her, Maggie's arm falls to the floor. A bottle of pills and a handwritten note spill from her tightly clutched palm.)

ANGIE. Maggie! No! What did you do?!

(She looks at the bottle of pills. Turns it upside down and shakes. Empty. She grabs Maggie's arm, feeling for a pulse. Nothing. Realizing what happened, Angie crumples to the floor beside the sofa. Heartbroken, unable to cry.)

ANGIE. Why, Maggie? It…it's just been a month… Why did you do it?

(Dale and Snyder slip softly back on stage, equally heartbroken.)

SNYDER. You should read the note.

ANGIE. I…I can't. A note like this deserves tears. Will you read it for me, Dale? Please?

(She holds the note in shaking fingers, as Dale kneels beside her. Reads over her shoulder.)

DALE. *(Reading.)* My dearest Angie…I never thought I would be writing a sentence like that…I've spent most of my post-prom life hating you. My only comfort was imagining how much I made you suffer. *(Turns to Angie.)* I can't read this anymore, sweetheart…

ANGIE. Please, Dale. I need to hear it.

DALE. *(Reading again. This is hard for him.)* My only comfort was imagining how much I made you suffer. But now that I've come to know you. Come to love you. Knowing that I caused you so much pain… tears me apart.

(Angie grabs Maggie's lifeless hand and holds it.)

DALE. *(Reading.)* This past month, you have made me so much happier than I deserve. I wish I could break this curse and free you, but I don't know how.

(Sligo and Waddy enter from different sides of the stage. They gather around Angie. Sharing her pain.)

DALE. *(Reading.)* Please forgive me. Because I can't forgive myself. All my love…Your wife-slash husband – slash – former enemy…

ANGIE. *(With pain.)* Oh, Maggie…

(Jared enters UL.)

JARED. What's up, dudes?

    (Crosses to the sofa. Looks at Maggie's arm flopped over.)

JARED. Whoa. She really is Saggy Maggie…

    (Angie groans.)

SNYDER. Can you be any more clueless?!

JARED. Uh, I dunno. I guess I could like, try…?

BLACKOUT

END OF ACT TWO, SCENE 2

ACT TWO
Scene 3

NARRATOR. Ah, Regret. That all-too-human capacity to take a single mistake and bludgeon ourselves with it for the rest of our lives. Others may give us an emotional kick in the chest now and then, but the deeper damage is how we choose to relive that pain or shame, over and over, for days or decades. Turning one foolish choice into a lifelong self-inflicted wound we jealously protect and never allow to heal.

Regret is the 'if only' disease unique to our species. If only things had been different. If only we hadn't said that or done that. If only we hadn't been as selfish, as scared, as cruel, or as blind. If only we had done more or walked away at the crucial moment. But that is like trying to reshape the wind. The past isn't perfect, and neither are we. Unless we can find a way to accept that, we can never truly live.

AT RISE: *Stage lights come up halfway, revealing the cemetery at night. A shimmer of silvery moonlight catches Angie, back against a tombstone, legs splayed in front of her. Half-empty bourbon bottles in each hand. She takes a long pull from each bottle and suddenly giggles. Waves it away, then hangs her head in drunken despair. After a moment, Maggie rises from behind one of the gravestones.)*

MAGGIE. What are you doing here, Angie? You, more than anyone, know we are not really here.

ANGIE. Oh, hi ya, Maggie Maggie.

MAGGIE. It's just Maggie.

ANGIE. Not when I'm seeing double! *(Giggles drunkenly and slaps her leg as she laughs.)* Oww!

MAGGIE. I have never seen you drunk before.

ANGIE. That makes us even. I've never seen you dead before! *(Laughs again and slaps her leg hard.)* Owww!

(Snyder rises from behind another tombstone.)

SNYDER. Oh, Angie…

ANGIE. Hey there, Snyder-roodle. Snicker-doodle. Slimy-poodle. *(Laughs again and slaps her leg hard.)* Owww. I should prob-ly stop doing that…

(Dale rises from behind a tombstone.)

DALE. You're hitting that bottle pretty hard.

ANGIE. Not as hard as I'm hitting my leg. *(Laughs again and slaps her leg hard.)* Owww. Bein' drunk hurts… *(Points to each one of them.)* I love you…and I love you…and I love you…

DALE. What are you doing, Angie?

ANGIE. Doooooing? What does it look like I'm dooooo-ing? I'm celebrating. It's my anniversary! *(Raises one of the bottles to the moon.)*

DALE. What anniversary?

ANGIE. Let me think a slecond… a seckel… *(She waves a finger to indicate 'one second.)* Today is my tenth anniversary with Juan-Carlos… Nineteen months since I first kissed Snyder-roony there…and three weeks since my Maggie Maggie died. *(Suddenly bitter.)* That enough anniversary for ya?! Huh?!

DALE. *(Gently.)* That's enough anniversaries for anyone, sweetheart.

ANGIE. But not for me! Thanks to my Maggie-girl's curse, I'm gonna be smoochin' and slayin' husbands 'til they run outta room to plant 'em! Old, young, rich, poor, fat, scrawny, bald hairy and chimp-like. I marry and bury 'em all. An equal opportunity destroyer. Right, Maggie Maggie?

(Jared rises from behind a tombstone.)

JARED. Dudes, like, you're having a party and didn't invite me?

ANGIE. S'not much of a party. It's pretty dead around here! Hahahaha *(Laughs again and slaps her leg hard.)* I am sooo not going to say 'Oww' this time. No, I'm not…

JARED. She's toasted.

ANGIE. Well, that would certainly explain why the gravestones are waltzing. *(Slaps Dale's leg.)* I'm a funny drunk.

SNYDER. You shouldn't be drinking so much, Angie.

ANGIE. I shouldn't be doing a lot of things. I shouldn't be loving. I shouldn't be losing. I shouldn't be kissing. I shouldn't be killing… I shouldn't be surviving…

DALE. That's no way to talk!

SNYDER. I think you're done, Angie…

ANGIE. *(Snapping.)* I'm not done! I wish I were done. I wish all this was over and I never had to hurt anybody again! Not have to see another funeral. Not have to put on another wedding ring. Not have to crawl home to an empty bed at night, knowing I was the one who made it empty. Least 'til the next poor sucker crosses lips with me!

DALE. It's not your fault, Angie.

ANGIE. Then whose fault is it?

DALE, JARED & SNYDER. *(Together. Pointing at Maggie.)* Hers!

MAGGIE. Oh, yeah. It's so easy to point fingers.

DALE. Dead fingers, thanks to you.

MAGGIE. Well, I have a finger for you too.

ANGIE. Not helping, people!

SNYDER. There's gotta be some way to break the curse.

ANGIE. One would thunk… one would thulenk… *(She waves a finger to indicate 'one second.)* Maybe if I kiss myself. *(Drunkenly tries to contort her lips to kiss herself.)* That's a lot harder than you might think…

DALE. There has to be a way.

ANGIE. I could have my lips removed?

SNYDER. Don't! I love those lips!

JARED. So do I.

ANGIE. I'm prob'ly the only one I know who shops 'Buy One – Get One Free' casket sales…

SNYDER. Come on, Maggie. Look at her! There has to be a curse cure. A spell check, or something?!

MAGGIE. You think I like this? Look at me. All I wanted was my Jared back… and I end up ghostly. And gay, I guess. You saw how my mother cried at our wedding. And that woman in Kentucky took forever to grant us a license.

ANGIE. (Singing drunkenly.)
*You made me love you
I didn't want to do it
Didn't' t want to do it*

(Angie laughs, then her head falls to her chest.)

ANGIE. I always hurt the ones I love. *(Muttering.)* Don't wanna hurt…anyone anymore…I don' wanna… hurt…no more…

(She slumps over, unconscious.)

MAGGIE. Oh, Angie…

(Sligo enters UL. Waddy following meekly behind.)

SLIGO. Hey, what's dollface doin' out here?

JARED. Celebrating.

SNYDER. Sligo, it's been a month. Where have you been?

SLIGO. A month? Man, time flies when you're six feet under. I took Stink-boy here with me to keep an eye on some of my old…uh, business associates. Man, you get a little dead, and your whole organization falls apart. Right, Stink-boy?

WADDY. Uh, right, Boss.

SLIGO. What's with the new broad?

SNYDER. Don't you recognize her? That's Maggie.

SLIGO. Saggy Maggie?

MAGGIE. I'm thirty-two years old and deceased. Isn't it time everyone stopped calling me by my high school nickname?!

SLIGO. That's right! You'se is the broad what put the evil eye on my Angie-girl! The dame what did this to me!

WADDY. To all of us.

SLIGO. Shut up, Stink-boy.

WADDY. You got it, Boss.

SLIGO. Why I oughtta…

MAGGIE. Bring it, you Scabface wannabe!

SLIGO. Scarface. Not Scabface. Don't you know your Pacino classics?

MAGGIE. You're dead. Scabface is just as appropriate.

SLIGO. Why, I oughtta..!

MAGGIE. What you outta do is stop saying 'Why, I oughtta…' A guy could get seriously smacked for that.

SLIGO. If you weren't a dame and I weren't dead, I'd…

MAGGIE. You'd what?!

(Angie sits up and screams.)

ANGIE. Stop it! Stop fighting! I can't take all of you arguing in my head! Day and night… Night and day…It's driving me…. driving me…

(Passes out again.)

SLIGO. See what you'se is doin' to my Angie-girl?!

MAGGIE. Me? Look what you're doing to my Angie!

SNYDER. Look what we are ALL doing to her! Two bottles of bourbon and passed out in a graveyard at midnight. We are killing her!

WADDY. One could make the point that she killed us first.

ALL. *(Together.)* Shut up, Stink-boy!

SNYDER. Look, we all love our wife. And none of us want to see her suffer like this. And Lord knows we don't need any more ex-husbands crowding around.

JARED. Especially since the last few have been such bottom-feeders.

(Sligo, Waddy and Maggie glare at him.)

JARED. I'm just sayin'.

SNYDER. It doesn't matter how we feel about each other. We all have to get along so she can keep it together.

DALE. I have an idea.

WADDY. Uh oh. Here we go again!

DALE. What do you mean?

JARED. It's not like your last couple of ideas turned out so great.

(They gesture to Maggie, then Sligo, without him noticing it.)

DALE. Oh, yeah. My bad.

SNYDER. So what's your big brainstorm this time?

DALE. Okay…We all agree that being her dead-husband harem is only making things worse for Angie. So if we really love her, there's only one thing we can do.

JARED. What's that?

DALE. An exorcism.

SNYDER. Are you brain-dead?! An exorcism would mean we go away…Go away to who knows where!

WADDY. Maybe hell.

SLIGO. Or worse.

MAGGIE. And we would never see our Angie again.

DALE. But she would be free of us. That'd make her hurt less. Isn't that worth a little suffering on our part?

WADDY. Or hell.

SLIGO. Or worse.

MAGGIE. I…I agree with Dale. If it's better for Angie, I say we go for it. No matter what happens to us.

(A pause, as they look at Angie passed out on a grave.)

SNYDER. So we're all in for this exorcism?

WADDY. Yes.

JARED. I guess.

DALE. 'Tis a far, far better thing…

SLIGO. *(Shrugs.)* What the hell.

WADDY. Or worse…

(They all exchange worried glances, as LIGHTS DIM. Suddenly, there is a BRIGHT FLASH.)

MAGGIE. Really? Lightning? As if the whole exorcism idea isn't scary enough?

BLACKOUT

END OF ACT TWO, SCENE 3

ACT TWO
Scene 4

(OVER DARKNESS)

DEMONIC VOICE #1: NYHAHAHAHA!

DEMONIC VOICE #2: I am a demon and I have possession of this woman's body!

DEMONIC VOICE #3: Her soul belongs to me!

DEMONIC VOICE #1: NYHAHAHA!

DEMONIC VOICE #2: You have no power over me!

DEMONIC VOICE #3: Angela is MINE!!!

DEMONIC VOICE #1: NYHAHAHAHAHAHAHAHA!

(Stage Lights FLASH suddenly. Angie is alone in the room. A photo of the Pope and crucifixes on the wall let us know we are now in the office of a Catholic priest.)

ANGIE. Cut it out, you guys! Stop fooling around.

(The church office is sparsely furnished in dark woods. A small table, covered with theological books, sits Center Stage. Stiff backed wooden chairs are positioned on both sides of it. Jared, Snyder and Dale enter, UL.)

SNYDER. Sorry, Ange. We couldn't resist.

DALE. We know how nervous you are. We were just trying to lighten the mood.

JARED. *The Exorcist* was like, my all-time favorite movie when I was a baby.

ANGIE. That explains a lot, Jared. But I still can't believe you guys talked me into this.

DALE. It may be the only way to break the curse.

ANGIE. Do you realize what could happen to you?

SNYDER. Speaking for the entire Angie Cadaver Club…we're willing to risk it, if there's even the slightest chance it frees you from this curse.

ANGIE. *(Choked up.)* I really love you, guys. All of you.

DALE. We love you too, sweetheart.

ANGIE. Now get out of here. I think I'll be less nervous if I talk to the priest alone.

SNYDER. Let's go, boys.

JARED. Good luck, Angie.

DALE. We're rooting for you.

ANGIE. Shoo! Someone's coming!

(The three ghosts scamper off DL, just as a FIGURE IN BLACK enters, UR. Angie whirls around to see a Nun in full classic habit. She immediately begins straightening up the upstage area, so we only see her back.)

NUN. Father Lawrence will be with you in a moment.

ANGIE. Thank you, Sister.

NUN. I heard voices. Who were you speaking to?

ANGIE. No one.

NUN. That's what they all say.

(The Nun moves closer, and reveals herself to be…)

ANGIE. Maggie?

NUN/MAGGIE. Sister Mary Margaret, actually.

ANGIE. I'm sorry. You look like someone I know. I knew.

NUN/MAGGIE. And who was that, dear?

ANGIE. My late husband. I mean, late wife. A friend, who, um cursed me.

NUN/MAGGIE. Father Lawrence is a counselor, dearie. He doesn't handle mental illness.

ANGIE. I'll keep that in mind.

NUN/MAGGIE. You do that.

>   *(After making sure the room is in meticulous order, the Nun casts a last doubtful look at Angie, then exits, UR. Angie crosses downstage nervously.)*

ANGIE. Good one, Angie. You tell a nun she looks like your dead husband. You really are losing it...

>   *(As she mutters to herself, FATHER LAWRENCE enters, UL. Even with his dark sunglasses, he looks like Sligo, only with a black clerical shirt and priest collar.)*

FATHER LAWRENCE. Hello?

ANGIE. Oh, hi, Father.

FATHER LAWRENCE. Who are you speaking to, my child?

ANGIE. I was just, um, talking to myself.

FATHER LAWRENCE. I see. My name is Father Lawrence Berg. Berg as in German, not Jewish.

ANGIE. I got that from the collar.

FATHER LAWRENCE. Of course.

>   *(The priest feels around for the table, then backs himself into the chair without removing his sunglasses.)*

ANGIE. You're blind.

FATHER LAWRENCE. Ah, that explains why I don't get much from these books! *(Smiles.)* That's a joke. Blind priests are allowed a modicum of humor. Please. Have a seat.

ANGIE. I'd rather pace, if you don't mind.

FATHER LAWRENCE. How can I help you, child?

ANGIE. I need an exorcism! Or an un-haunting or de-spiriting. Whatever you guys do here.

FATHER LAWRENCE. I am afraid you have seen too many movies. The church does not do that kind of thing on a regular basis.

ANGIE. Who does?

FATHER LAWRENCE. Do you feel you are possessed?

ANGIE. No. I just see my husband way too much.

FATHER LAWRENCE. Well, marriage counseling is something we do a great deal of. Where is your husband these days?

ANGIE. Here. In this room.

FATHER LAWRENCE. Oh?

ANGIE. In your chair.

FATHER LAWRENCE. Sorry?

ANGIE. When I look at you, I see Sligo.

FATHER LAWRENCE. *(Confused.)* Is this Sligo a man of the cloth?

ANGIE. No. Although he did have a lot to do with funerals.

FATHER LAWRENCE. And he looks like me?

ANGIE. It's hard to tell. I don't know what you look like.

FATHER LAWRENCE. I'm afraid you have other issues that may require more help than I can offer...

ANGIE. No, it's just that I can't see your real face. To me, you look like my husband.

FATHER LAWRENCE. Sligo?

ANGIE. My ex.

FATHER LAWRENCE. You are divorced then?

ANGIE. I wish. No, Sligo is dead.

FATHER LAWRENCE. You are a widow.

ANGIE. Repeatedly.

FATHER LAWRENCE. *(Takes a drink of water.)* You've been married and widowed before?

ANGIE. A few times.

FATHER LAWRENCE. How many is a few?

ANGIE. Eighteen.

FATHER LAWRENCE. *(Spits his water.)* Did you say eighteen?!

ANGIE. Sorry, I meant seventeen. A few looked so much alike, it's easy to lose track.

FATHER LAWRENCE. I see.

ANGIE. You do?

FATHER LAWRENCE. Actually I can't see. I was speaking metaphorically. Please continue.

ANGIE. The only ones who don't look like my dead husbands are the ones who are about to be my next husbands. Who will then become my next ex-husbands within three months.

FATHER LAWRENCE. When they die.

ANGIE. It's not very considerate of them. Leaving me alone like that.

FATHER LAWRENCE. Until the next future dead husband comes along?

ANGIE. You do see!

FATHER LAWRENCE. In truth, I am somewhat glad I don't. Perhaps we should start at the beginning?

ANGIE. Okay…When I was back in high school, there was this girl, Saggy Maggie we called her, because her face always seemed to drag down.

FATHER LAWRENCE. *(Nodding.)* Saggy Maggie. Go on.

ANGIE. She never had a boyfriend until this one guy asked her out. They went steady for five months, then he asked her to the prom.

FATHER LAWRENCE. So Saggy Maggie was happy?

ANGIE. Until she caught me kissing him. I didn't mean to. Actually I did, but that's why she put a curse on me.

FATHER LAWRENCE. The church does not believe in curses.

ANGIE. Neither did I. At least until husband number six. Then I started to detect a pattern.

FATHER LAWRENCE. A quick learner, I see.

ANGIE. Maggie told me that since I kissed her boyfriend, I could have him. But that everyone I kissed I would only have for a short time. Now whenever a guy sees me, he has an overwhelming urge to kiss me. We get married, and then within three months, he dies.

FATHER LAWRENCE. And how do your multitude of ex-husbands die?

ANGIE. The usual ways. Sneeze and crack their skulls on a urinal. Brush their teeth with Ben Gay. Wear a Halloween costume into a bank and get shot by a security guard.

FATHER LAWRENCE. I'm not sure those are the usual ways.

ANGIE. I guess not. But within three months they're dead. Fortunately, I've learned how much of a blessing life insurance can be.

FATHER LAWRENCE. You take out policies on each husband?

ANGIE. Wouldn't you? We usually do about ten million. More than that raises suspicion.

FATHER LAWRENCE. So you are both deadly and wealthy.

ANGIE. Somewhere in the neighborhood of two hundred and sixty million.

FATHER LAWRENCE. Nice neighborhood.

ANGIE. Anyway, after I married Maggie…

FATHER LAWRENCE. Saggy Maggie?

ANGIE. Yes.

FATHER LAWRENCE. Saggy Maggie who cursed you?

ANGIE. Messed up, I know. That's why I need your help.

FATHER LAWRENCE. Because you married the woman who cursed you back in high school?

ANGIE. It's okay. She's dead now. Not that that's okay, but it's why they decided I needed an exorcism.

FATHER LAWRENCE. Who decided?

ANGIE. My ex-husbands. And Maggie.

FATHER LAWRENCE. I thought they were all dead?

ANGIE. They are. But that doesn't mean they stop telling me what to do. You know how men are. And Maggie. Why are you smiling?

FATHER LAWRENCE. I suddenly thought of a subject for my next article in *Abnormal Psychology Today*.

ANGIE. Honestly, Father. I'm not crazy. I'm cursed. Doomed to be kissed and married, over and over.

FATHER LAWRENCE. Have you ever thought of simply saying no?

ANGIE. I tried. But they become obsessed. We both do. You know how hard it is to resist someone who finds you irresistible.

FATHER LAWRENCE. Not really. Celibate and all that.

ANGIE. I'm sorry.

FATHER LAWRENCE. So am I, it seems…

ANGIE. Can you help me, Father?

FATHER LAWRENCE. Tell me, child. Are you a serial killer?

ANGIE. That's what the police thought. Especially this one detective. He tracked me for years, convinced I was offing my exes. But it's hard to say I was responsible when someone spills one hundred proof whiskey on their shorts, and they catch fire when they stand too close to the barbecue grill.

FATHER LAWRENCE. I can imagine…No, actually, I can't.

ANGIE. Usually the cause of death is so silly, they can't charge me. But this one detective refused to give up.

FATHER LAWRENCE. What happened to him?

ANGIE. Snyder? He was husband number thirteen. The one in Baggage Hold when I met Dale. It's always within three months. Then I start waiting for the axe to fall. Like with Luther.

FATHER LAWRENCE. What happened to Luther?

ANGIE. The axe fell. He worked in the garden department of Home Depot. There was a cleanup in aisle eleven that day. Believe me.

FATHER LAWRENCE. Strangely enough, I think I do.

(Narrator enters, UL, as Angie and the priest mime a conversation.)

NARRATOR. Now you may be wondering how our Father Lawrence could resist the curse. First, there was his collar and his vows. Secondly, the fact that he was blind proved a real blessing. He still felt an undeniable urge to kiss her…

(The priest rises, his lips puckering wildly.)

NARRATOR. But since he couldn't actually see the object of his affection, Angie was able to sidestep his advances…

(Father Lawrence wanders the room, kissing at thin air. Angie manages to keep a distance between them.)

NARRATOR. …at least until the urge passed, and they both remembered his collar and his vows.

(Father Lawrence regains control of his lips. Feels his way back to his chair. Then collapses. Angie does the same.)

ANGIE. That was close.

FATHER LAWRENCE. I am glad to see you have developed a greater sense of self-control, my child. *(Wiping his brow.)* Even if I haven't…

ANGIE. I owe it all to these talks of ours. These last few months of counseling have helped me so much.

FATHER LAWRENCE. I am pleased to hear it.

NARRATOR. And so Angie got her exercise, if not her exorcism. And as their conversations continued every Friday, week after week, Angie felt Maggie's curse exerting less and less power over her life.

(Narrator exits, DR.)

ANGIE. I had another close call today, Father.

FATHER LAWRENCE. Would you like to tell me about it?

ANGIE. I was at the dentist's office, and when I opened my mouth, the horny old goat tried to kiss me.

FATHER LAWRENCE. Did you do the Twelve Step Program we discussed?

ANGIE. Yes. I kicked him in the crotch. Took Twelve Steps toward the door…then ran like hell!

FATHER LAWRENCE. I'm proud of you.

ANGIE. *(Smiling.)* I'm kind of proud of me too. It was a pretty impressive kick.

FATHER LAWRENCE. *(Gently.)* Angela…Have you ever considered the possibility that you are not merely the victim of this supposed curse, but may also be helping it along?

ANGIE. Are you serious?

FATHER LAWRENCE. I seem to be. This is my serious face.

ANGIE. How can you think I would want this? That anybody would? Men fall in love with me. And I fall in love with them, time and time again.

FATHER LAWRENCE. Sounds terrible. Especially for a young girl, who was heartbroken because nobody would take her to the prom.

ANGIE. That was fifteen years and seventeen husbands ago! *(Turns away.)* I'm not her anymore.

FATHER LAWRENCE. That is precisely my point. You are no longer that frightened, fragile little girl. You are an intelligent, independent, extremely desirable woman, with the ability to get any man she wants with just a kiss. Who also happens to be wealthy beyond belief. Almost a fairy tale come true, wouldn't you say?

ANGIE. Except that I have lost every person I have ever loved!

FATHER LAWRENCE. Have you? The way you talk, all your exes are still around. Watching over you. Talking to you every day. Hardly what we consider closure.

ANGIE. Yes, but…

FATHER LAWRENCE. You have the best of both worlds. Lots of people who love you, and not one who can ever leave. Perhaps it's not the curse holding them to you. Preventing them from crossing over. Maybe it's you.

ANGIE. Me? You think I'm doing this?

FATHER LAWRENCE. You cling to the past so desperately, because you feel your past is all that defines you.

(Dale enters UL.)

DALE. He has a point, sweetheart.

ANGIE. What?

DALE. I said, he has a point.

(SNYDER enters from UR.)

SNYDER. I never thought I'd say this, but Dale is right.

ANGIE. You think so?

(Maggie enters from DL.)

MAGGIE. We all do.

ANGIE. I am the one holding you here? Keeping you from crossing over?

(Waddy & Jared enter from DR.)

WADDY. Yes.

ANGIE. And you all knew that?

JARED. Like, ever since day one.

ANGIE. Then why didn't you say something? Why didn't you tell me?

SNYDER. It was something you needed to find out on your own.

FATHER LAWRENCE. They are here. In this room, aren't they?

ANGIE. You can see them?

FATHER LAWRENCE. Clearly not. But when one loses sight, the other senses are often enhanced. I can feel some sort of…presence in the room. Like a chill, or a tingle. *(Points in the general direction of each.)* I feel it coming from there…and there…and there, there and there…

ANGIE. That's Waddy, Jared, Maggie, Dale and Snyder. *(Looking at each one fondly.)* My spouses. My loves…

FATHER LAWRENCE. And the rest? The other twelve?

ANGIE. They are more shy. Or sad. I can't always see them, but I can feel them in my heart. I always can.

FATHER LAWRENCE. And how does that make you feel?

DALE. Tell him, Sweetheart.

ANGIE. I…I don't know…

MAGGIE. Tell him, Angie.

FATHER LAWRENCE. How does it make you feel?

ANGIE. Loved….Safe…

SNYDER. And..?

ANGIE. *(Softly.)* Not alone...

DALE. Oh, sweetheart…

FATHER LAWRENCE. All love is desperate. We all cling so tightly because with each hug, we know that we will have to let go some day. We care, realizing that one day we will cry. We love, knowing deep down inside, we will eventually lose.

SNYDER. Listen to him, Angie.

FATHER LAWRENCE. That is the glorious sadness of it all. The best we can ever hope for is to steal as many moments from the universe as we can.

ANGIE. But that's terrible.

FATHER LAWRENCE. On the contrary. That's love. It is what makes finding it so very precious. *(Pause.)* I have given the matter a great deal of thought. What if I were to tell you that I could end your curse once and for all? End it today.

ANGIE. You can?

FATHER LAWRENCE. I can't. But I believe you can. It is my experience that curses fade over time. And you are now strong enough to overcome yours. But to do so, you will have to let go of all the ghosts of old lovers.

ANGIE. That's easier said than done.

FATHER LAWRENCE. True. The past is a comfort, but it also imprisons us. Let go of the past, my child. What are you afraid of?

ANGIE. I don't know.

FATHER LAWRENCE. I believe you do.

MAGGIE. Tell him, Angie.

SNYDER. Tell him what you are afraid of.

FATHER LAWRENCE. What are you afraid of?

ANGIE. I don't know.

DALE. Yes, you do, sweetheart. Deep down inside, you know.

FATHER LAWRENCE. What are you really afraid of?

ANGIE. *(Desperately.)* That it's not the curse! That it's me! As long as the curse is there, I have an excuse for being lonely and unhappy. Unable to have a long lasting relationship. But once the curse is lifted…

FATHER LAWRENCE. There are no guarantees in life.

ANGIE. I know. And that terrifies me. I've been married so many times, but what if…what if I really don't know how to love?

FATHER LAWRENCE. What else are you afraid of?

MAGGIE. Tell him, Angie.

WADDY. Tell him.

DALE. You can do it, sweetheart.

ANGIE. I'm afraid…that I need the curse. That without it…no one will ever love me. That I'll end up alone. Completely alone.

SNYDER. Oh, Angie.

FATHER LAWRENCE. It's frightening, I know. But you have to let them go. And if they love you, they will let you go too. Then the curse will lose its power over you.

DALE. Wait a minute? You mean, that's it? That's all there is to it?

MAGGIE. Sounds about right.

WADDY. Some witch you are!

MAGGIE. Hey, I was new at this, remember?

JARED. *(Crossing to her side.)* Give her a break, man. Maggie's suffered enough.

MAGGIE. Thanks, Jared.

JARED. Like no problem, witchy woman.

MAGGIE. Witchy woman. You haven't called me that since high school.

(She takes his hand. Smiles up at him,)

JARED. Whoa! Dramatic plot shift.

MAGGIE. *(Giggles.)* I know!

FATHER LAWRENCE. So what do you say, Angela? Are you ready to let them all go? To say goodbye to the ghosts of old lovers?

ANGIE. I'm not sure I can. I…I'm not sure I want to.

FATHER LAWRENCE. If you want to move forward, you have to bid them goodbye.

SNYDER. It's time, Angie.

DALE. You have to let us go.

ANGIE. But what will you do? Where will you go?

MAGGIE. Who knows? Move on to the next plane of existence. Whatever that is.

ANGIE. And you're okay with that?

ALL EXES. *(Together.)*. Yes.

ANGIE. *(Takes a deep breath.)*. So…how do I do this?

FATHER LAWRENCE. Just decide the past has no more power over you. Then say goodbye.

DALE. You can do it, sweetheart.

WADDY. We're ready, Angie.

SNYDER. It's time.

ANGIE. Okay, here goes…

(She slowly crosses to each one in turn, through the following.)

ANGIE. Goodbye, Waddy.

WADDY. Goodbye, Angie.

ANGIE. Stay fresh.

WADDY. Ha! Good one.

(Waddy steps backward, tears in his eyes, as if he's being pulled away by an unseen force. He blows Angie a kiss, then exits, UL. Angie crosses to Jared and Maggie, who are holding hands like two teenagers in love.)

ANGIE. Look at you two. Back together again.

MAGGIE. I guess there is love after death.

JARED. Cool! You think I'll like, see any of those Victoria Secret angels? *(She punches his shoulder.)* Kidding! I'm kidding! Owww.

ANGIE. *(To Maggie.)* So, Maggie…Are we good?

MAGGIE. We're good. Sorry about the whole, terrible curse, murder your husbands and ruin your life thingie.

ANGIE. About that…

JARED. We should like, go, Maggie. I wanna see those purply gates.

MAGGIE. Pearly gates.

JARED. Dude, you are soooo much smarter than me!

(They look to Angie with sudden sadness, then slowly step backwards, until they too exit, DR. Dale crosses to her, clearly heartbroken.)

DALE. Goodbye, Sweetheart.

ANGIE. Goodbye, Dale. I'm sorry I cut your life short, and you never got a chance to fulfill your dreams.

DALE. That's okay. There are dreams, and then there are the left turns life throws at us. You were one side trip I'm glad I didn't miss out on. Three months with you as my wife was better than a lifetime without you.

ANGIE. I will always love you.

DALE. I'll always love you, too. With or without the curse.

ANGIE. Thanks. I needed that.

DALE. Well, gotta fly! Which I guess is full circle, because we met in an airport. *(Reaches for her, their hands almost touching.)* Take care of yourself, my precious wife.

ANGIE. I'll try.

DALE. Can I say one more thing?

ANGIE. What's that?

DALE. *(Pumping his fist in the air.)* Top ten!

(He too is pulled backwards. Before he exits, UR, he places a comforting hand on Snyder, who is trying desperately to hold back his own tears. Snyder nods a farewell to Dale, then crosses to Angie.)

SNYDER. The uh, others asked me to say goodbye for them. Most had a lot of eternal rest they needed to catch up on. Truth is husbands Two through Twelve were too choked up to say goodbye. The crybabies.

ANGIE. I get it. I'll miss them though. And I think I'll miss you most of all, Scarecrow.

SNYDER. Yeah? Well no need to get all mushy faced about it. I'll just be over the rainbow whenever you need me. You gonna be okay? I mean, now that the band is breaking up.

ANGIE. The band?

SNYDER. Angie and her Exes. We had quite a run.

ANGIE. Yeah, we did. *(Wiping her eyes.)* Look at me. I'm crying. I'm really crying.

SNYDER. It's about damn time. You take care of yourself, sweetie. I'll see you on the other side.

ANGIE. If they let me in. I got a lot to make up for.

SNYDER. They will. Wish I could kiss you goodbye.

ANGIE. Me, too. Next life, okay?

SNYDER. It's a date, beautiful.

(Snyder is pulled backwards, then slowly exits, DL. Angie collapses in her chair and sobs quietly. Grateful for the tears that were so long in coming.)

FATHER LAWRENCE. I sense they are all gone now.

ANGIE. Yes.

FATHER LAWRENCE. And how do you feel?

ANGIE. Alone... Scared... and free.

FATHER LAWRENCE. Welcome to adulthood.

ANGIE. Thank you, Father.

    (Suddenly the light illuminating the priest turns BLUE. He takes off his sunglasses. Stands and says, in Sligo's voice...)

FATHER LAWRENCE/SLIGO. Least I could do, dollface.

ANGIE. Sligo?

FATHER LAWRENCE/SLIGO. Thought I'd jump into the old priest's body for a sec. You didn't think I'd leave without saying goodbye to you'se?

ANGIE. You know, for a bad guy, you're not really a bad man.

FATHER LAWRENCE/SLIGO. Maybe. But don't spread it around. I got me a reputation to uphold, ya follow? So why not kiss me goodbye. Give the old Father a thrill.

ANGIE. Isn't that dangerous?

FATHER LAWRENCE/SLIGO. Hey, Danger is my middle name.

ANGIE. I thought it was Leslie?

FATHER LAWRENCE/SLIGO. Don't tell anyone that either. My rep, ya follow? Now gimme a smooch, dollface.

    (She kisses him. The BLUE LIGHT slowly fades. Father Lawrence assumes his milder stance.)

FATHER LAWRENCE. Uh… Angela…

ANGIE. Oh, I'm sorry, Father.

FATHER LAWRENCE. *(Sits. Reaches for his sunglasses.)* That was awkward.

ANGIE. Sligo made me do it.

FATHER LAWRENCE. Be that as it may, I believe we are done here. Go and find love on your own. You don't need the curse anymore.

ANGIE. Thank you, Father.

    (She moves to exit, DL. Suddenly, she turns toward him.)

ANGIE. Wait a minute. I kissed you!

The KISS ME Curse

FATHER LAWRENCE. Something neither of us will ever mention again.

ANGIE. Don't you feel an irresistible urge to marry me?

FATHER LAWRENCE. I can marry you. But as a priest. Not as a husband. The collar, remember?

ANGIE. *(Beat, then…)*. And I don't love you at all! That's awesome!

FATHER LAWRENCE. That seems to be a definition of awesome I have yet to encounter.

ANGIE. The curse is over! I'm free!

FATHER LAWRENCE. Thank heavens. Now go forth in love, my child.

ANGIE. I will. Thank you, Father!

(She gives him a kiss on the cheek, then exits happily. Father Lawrence looks up.)

FATHER LAWRENCE. Forgive me, Lord, for I have sinned…But wow! What a kisser!

(He staggers off UL, as Narrator enters, UR.)

NARRATOR. And that's the story of the 'Kiss Me' Curse. Last we heard, Angie had moved back to Pewee Valley looking for true love. She has kissed three different men over the past six months and not one of them died…which made the insurance companies and local police force very happy. Angie is currently listed on an online dating site. And with two hundred and sixty-five million in the bank, I doubt she will have any trouble meeting people.

The moral of our story? Let go of all the fears and failures of your past. Cherish those who are in your life now. And turn to the person beside you and kiss them like you really mean it.

(He points to someone in the audience.)

NARRATOR. Uh, not her, Mr. Frisky Hands. The woman you brought with you. We've seen enough death tonight.

NARRATOR. Oh, and if your husband, wife or significant other never got a chance to go to their high school Prom…take them home tonight. Dress up fancy, put on some oldie's music, and slow dance like awkward teenagers.

Believe me, they will love you forever…

(He blows the audience a kiss, then exits, UR.)

CURTAIN

The End

The KISS ME Curse

ORIGINAL CAST

Narrator/Mr. LaGrange	Allen Schuyler
Angie Buckner	Tiffany Smith
Dale Watterson	R. Wayne Hogue, Jr.
Snyder/Waiter #2	Tim Gooch
Jared	Simeon Burks
Maggie/Sister Mary Margaret	Candace Kresse
Waddy Peytona/Waiter #1	Rick Fletcher
Sligo Newcastle/Father Lawrence	Beau Solley
Director	Vin Morreale, Jr.
Stage Manager	Erika Wardlow
Lighting Designer	Charles Wade
Follow Spot	Mandy Michelle
Set Design	Bill Baker
Set Construction	Bob & Jane Burke
LCP Board Liaison	Teresa Wentzel

The KISS ME Curse was originally commissioned by the Little Colonel Playhouse of Kentucky to open their 60th Season. Many character names are based on locations leading to the theater.

LaGrange, *Buckner* and *Lawrenceburg* are neighboring cities.
Watterson and *Snyder* are the names of area freeways.
Both *Waddy Peytona* and *Sligo Newcastle* are actual highway exits, their signs still visible driving to the theater.

VIN MORREALE, JR.

About The Author

Vin Morreale, Jr. is an award-winning screenwriter, acting teacher, casting director and internationally produced playwright.

Vin was a founding member of the San Francisco Playwrights Center and the Senseless Bickering Comedy Theatre. He has directed hundreds of works for stage, screen and radio across the country.

As president of *Vin Morreale Casting*, along with his nationally known *Burning Up The Stage* acting workshops, he has helped nearly 30,000 actors find work in movies, TV, stage and video.

Vin was awarded the prestigious *Al Smith Writing Fellowship*, and his scripts, stage plays, documentaries, museum exhibits and radio comedy have received hundreds of productions around the world, as well as being translated into Chinese, Italian, Russian and Spanish.

Vin has sold material to network and cable television networks, had screenplays optioned and produced, and his work has been seen in more than 15 countries. He was named a top screenwriter by both The International Screenwriters Association and TheBlacklist.org.

You can find more of his books at *academyartspress.com*.

THE KISS ME CURSE

Also by Vin Morreale, Jr.

ACADEMY ARTS PRESS
academyartspress.com/titles
300 Monologues
150 Acting Scenes
Two Character Chaos
The Carrie Variations
All My Passions
A Day At The White House: The Sparx Brothers Go To Washington
Knowing When To Leave
Dark Wilderness & Other Stories
Mabel The Maple
Too Many Rules

DRAMATIC PUBLISHING
dramaticpublishing.com/authors/profile/view/url/vin-morreale-jr
Burning Up The Stage — *Monologues & Audition Scenes for Actors from 6 to 70*
Breaking & Entering
Uncool
Nicky's Secret
The Happy Holidays Collection
Southern Discomfort
House of The Seven Gables

ELDRIDGE PUBLISHING
histage.com/search?q=Morreale
The Fairyland Detective Agency
Sonoma White & The Seven Dolts
Fairies, Fantasies & Just Plain Fun

OFF THE WALL PUBLISHING
offthewallplays.com
Exquisite Anxieties
Forsaken
Temp Work
Ladies Guild Pre-Christmas Planning Session
Captive Christmas

www.ingramcontent.com/pod-product-compliance
Lightning Source LLC
Chambersburg PA
CBHW050439010526
44118CB00013B/1596